Seeing God in the
Life of David the King

CHALLENGE
BIBLE STUDY GUIDES

Old Testament Women by Sara Buswell
Believers or Beguilers
Courageous Overcomers
Vain or Visionary
Selfless or Selfish

When God Calls by Sara Buswell
Responding to God's Call
Submitting to God's Call

The Life of David by Mary Nelle Schaap
Seeing God in the Life of Young David
Seeing God in the Life of David the King

Portraits of Jesus from the Gospel Writers by Mary Nelle Schaap
Portraits of Jesus from Matthew and Mark
Portraits of Jesus from Luke and John

Studies in Old Testament Poetry by Kathleen Buswell Nielson
This God We Worship
Resting Secure

Seeing God in the Life of David the King

Mary Nelle Schaap

Baker Books

A Division of Baker Book House Co.
Grand Rapids, Michigan 49516

Copyright 1993 by Mary Nelle Schaap

Published by Baker Books
a Division of Baker Book House Company
P.O. Box 6287, Grand Rapids, Michigan 49516-6287

ISBN: 0-8010-8348-6

Printed in the United States of America

Chapters in this compilation are taken from *David's Lord* © 1989 by Baker
Book House Company

Contents

Foreword

avid's life and writings have been a powerful force in my life since I was a child. I can hear my dad's voice as he read Psalm 103 to the family after my brother was killed in England in a plane crash during World War II.

When as a teenager I enthusiastically gave my life to the Lord at a Bible conference on a mountain in North Carolina, someone wisely suggested to me that I worship God each morning with a psalm. I found doing so gave me words with which to praise and prayers to pray.

I discovered my attitude would change along with David's as I worked through a psalm. Discouragement changed to hope and anticipation of what God would do next, resentments changed to forgiveness, and depression to joy.

I was able to grasp the comfort God had for me when there was sorrow, and strength when things were too tough for me to handle.

Subtle sins were pointed out, but David's prayers of confession and his acceptance of God's complete cleansing often led me from guilt into a sense of restoration.

Perhaps what helped me most, however, was that through David I learned to worship. I found myself centering my mind and heart on God and on his character, instead of on myself or on horizontal relationships. I found, as David would put it, that I was choosing to "delight myself in the Lord." Following David's life and reading the thoughts and emotions he articulated in the psalms revealed to me a man who knew God and who constantly drew from the well of God's character.

While I was a sophomore in Wheaton College, blithesomely going about my affairs without a care in the world, I was called to the dean's office one day to take a phone call. My world crashed around me, for it was to inform me that my father, while on the scaffolding of a building he had designed, had stepped on a loose board, fallen to the cement below, and was critically injured.

As I was on the long and lonely train ride home to be with my family, I went into the rest room, knelt down on a little sofa that was there, and poured out my stunned heart to God. I took the Book of Psalms in hope that through them God would say something to me so I could function.

He did! My eyes fell on these words: "The steps of a good man are ordered by the LORD" (Ps. 37:23 KJV). These words were as real to me as though God had sent an angel or I had heard his voice. Something happened to me that day. An awareness came to me that has been growing and continuing ever since: that God wanted to minister personally to my needs, and that his plan was to use the words of Scripture to do it.

Many, many other examples were to follow, when God used his Word to teach me and show me what he was like, especially through the life and psalms of David. These Bible passages present not only the historical events of David's life, his good and bad experiences, but David's psalms also present his inner reactions, his thoughts and emotions, what was going on in his mind.

In the companion study, *Seeing God in the Life of Young David,* we look at questions such as: How on earth could a fresh young shepherd boy challenge a giant who had terrified the whole army of Israel from the king on down? How could he lead his troops to rout the powerful Philistines over and over? How could he endure Saul's cruelties without bitterness or resentment? In this study we want to discover: How could he rule with such grace and skill? How could he feel totally forgiven and restored after his horrendous sin with Bathsheba?

Two threads run through the historical records of David's life and also through his psalms: the heart of God, and the heart of David.

> [Samuel said,] "The LORD has sought out a man after his own heart, and appointed him leader of his people" (1 Sam. 13:14). The LORD said to Samuel [at David's anointing to be king] . . . "The LORD does not look at the things man looks at. Man looks at the outward appearance, but God looks at the heart" (1 Sam. 16:7).

Paul said that God himself described David in this way: "I have found David son of Jesse a man after my own heart; he will do everything I want him to do" (Acts 13:22). What does the phrase *a man after God's own heart* mean? Many have written about it, and yet its precise meaning is still somewhat elusive. Does it refer to the fact that David longed for God, and sought him with his whole heart? Does it mean that David had a heart that pleased God, and therefore God had a special love for him? Does it mean David had a heart patterned after God's heart?

Perhaps all of these meanings are encompassed in the phrase. I am convinced that God saw in David a man who could understand him as few men have. He could reveal things to David about himself, and David would catch what God was saying. David's heart responded to God's heart, and yet the closeness never caused David to forget God's majesty and greatness, or to lose sight of the fact that God was the one and only holy sovereign Lord, while David was a mere creature. As God's traits and attributes were carved into David's mind, they became a part of his innermost being, and God could mold David's mind and heart so that he could grasp for himself the beauties of God's character and communicate them to others.

David was not perfect; his failures are faithfully recorded. He was, nevertheless, used by God throughout the Bible as a sort of standard—a measuring stick for others in their relationships with God. It seems to me the reason for this is that David's driving purpose was to get to know God, to please him, and to be the person God intended him to be, inside and out. Like the needle on a compass that always points north, David's heart always turned back to God, and everything in his life was related to God. When David sinned, he recognized that it was against God. When he managed to be righteous, it was because God had given him his Spirit within. When he used bad judgment, it was because he had not sought God's wisdom. Wasn't that the beauty of David's life? His heart was open to God, and the direction of his heart and life was always toward God.

This study is designed to help you delve into the life of David as he learned to know God and relied on what he knew of God. We will try to discover some of the reasons David was so loved and honored by God. One of the last things David told his son Solomon before he turned over the throne to him was this: "[Know] the God of your father. . . . If you seek him, he will be found by you" (1 Chron.

28:9). My prayer is that you will come to a new understanding of the attributes of God and a new joy in getting
to know him through this study. As we seek to do this with
all our hearts, we will grow more and more to be men and
women "after God's own heart."

Study Plan

1. Read the questions at the beginning of each lesson.

2. Read the Scripture passage(s) listed and be aware of the questions as you read. Allow time to think about words or phrases or incidents that are especially meaningful to you. Underline them in your Bible.

3. Formulate initial answer(s) to questions.

4. If possible, discuss answers with a friend or group.

5. Read the lesson commentary.

6. Revise answers, if necessary.

7. Apply your answers to your life as God directs.

1

God Crowns David, the Successful Leader

Primary Scripture Reading

2 Samuel 1–6, 8–10

Supplementary References

Proverbs 3:5, 6
Psalm 32, 20, 21, 105
Mark 10:42–45

Questions for Study and Discussion

1. In 2 Samuel 1 the news of Saul's death came to David. What would be the normal reaction to the death of such a destructive and evil king?

   What was David's reaction?

   In David's revered poem in this chapter, "The Lament of the Bow," pick out the graphic expressions that have become common in our language. Which lines strike you as the most beautiful and moving?

   How would this tribute endear David to Israel?

2. Read 2 Samuel 2:1–7. What was the first thing David did after he had honored Saul and Jonathan (2:1, 2)?

How did this exemplify what his son Solomon wrote in Proverbs 3:5, 6?

What impresses you about the way David proceeded?

What was his first recorded act as king (2:5–7)?

3. Read 2 Samuel 2:8–3:39. Explain the tensions between David's followers and the house of Saul.

   What kind of man was Abner?

   How did Joab thwart David's carefully laid efforts at peace?

   How might David's struggle with Saul's house (extended family) have been easier if David's men had possessed his standards?

4. How did David regard Abner's death?

   Did David's punishment of Joab fit the crime?

   Read 2 Samuel 4. How did Ish-Bosheth's assassins expect David to react, do you think?

   How did David repay them? How must all the people of Israel, not just Judah, have regarded this new kind of king (see 3:36)?

5. When the tribes of Israel united under David (2 Sam. 5:1–5), what was their attitude toward him?

What qualities in David do you see that made Israel more ready to accept him as king?

Read 2 Samuel 5 and note David's accomplishments. What was the significance of making Jerusalem the capital city?

Why was it important to have the ark of the covenant brought to Jerusalem?

6. When David met his first military crisis as king (2 Sam. 5:17–25), where did he go for help?

   What was the outcome?

   Read 2 Samuel 8 (note: chronologically 2 Samuel 8 follows 2 Samuel 5). Locate the places on a map to get a picture of how David was extending all borders. How does the Bible account for David's success at making Israel a great power (5:10, 12, 25, and 8:6, 14)?

7. List David's traits that made him an excellent leader. Explain how these are good for anyone in a leadership position.

   Read Mark 10:42–45. What was Christ's description of leadership?

   How did David show the people what God was like?

   List the characteristics of God you see in these chapters.

A beautiful sight is Canada geese flying in a V-formation against a blue sky. The leader, we are told, works very hard, flapping its wings vigorously and creating an airstream for the other geese. Those in the back have an easier time of it, flying in the draft, but the leader soon tires, goes to the back, and another takes over. They can thus cover an amazing number of miles. Leadership in the body of believers is much like that. For a time, the person out front has to work very hard, making it easier for the others; then another takes over the lead with new strength and vigor, and the former leader takes the role of follower. A great deal can be done in this way, but the leader in front is vital.

When Saul was fatally wounded in battle at Mount Gilboa and then fell on his own sword, the time had come for David to take his place as leader of Israel. David was an excellent leader and could inspire people to "fly in formation" with him. The first ten chapters of 2 Samuel cover about the first twenty years of David's reign and relate David's amazing successes and triumphs in establishing Israel as a nation. As we study his leadership, we see many reasons why he was so effective. This may inspire and help us to be more effective in the leadership responsibilities and circles of influence we have.

Close to fifteen years had passed since Samuel had visited David's father Jesse's house, having been told by God that David would eventually be king of Israel. That account ended, "So Samuel took the horn of oil and anointed him in the presence of his brothers, and from that day on the Spirit of the LORD came upon David in power" (1 Sam. 16:13). David did not become king for many years. But, as we reviewed his life in the study *Seeing God in the Life of Young David*, we marveled at his consciousness of God's presence. He knew he had been guarded and protected physically, that he had been supplied with strength and stamina when ordinarily he would have collapsed and given up on his own. He was aware that he had been given faith and encouragement when his spirit was weak and his faith wavering.

Now Saul had died, and one might expect that David would be eager to take over the throne and rule Israel in the way it should be ruled. We admire David immensely for showing he could wait patiently for God to direct. God used this time to hone his abilities and qualities, so that he was ready to be an excellent leader from the first.

Setting the Standard

From the very beginning David set a high moral tone. His first priority was to honor Saul and Jonathan as a king and a prince should be honored. One might think that David would have had some sense of relief and pleasure that God had finally removed that evil and destructive despot, but if there was anything other than deep sorrow in David's heart, it is not recorded. Saul's insane cruelty to David was well known; but when David paid his beautiful, sincere tribute to the man who had brought him so much suffering, how the people must have admired him! His song for Saul, "The Lament of the Bow," is a very moving and beautiful piece of literature. True, it was also a lament for his beloved friend Jonathan, but David honored Saul as God would have liked Saul to be and a king of Israel should be. The death of Jonathan was a great blow to David. He had probably assumed that Jonathan would be at his side when he became king, would help him make peace with the Benjamites, Saul's tribe, and would be a close companion and confidant who would give him advice and encouragement. How much better Jonathan would have been than Joab, but this was not to be.

It was apparent to those nearby that David took over as king with a heavy heart but also with a clear conscience. He had done nothing to precipitate Saul's death, nor had he engineered or manipulated events to hurry the process. What a beautiful way to begin, to know in his own heart that, in all those thirteen or fourteen years since his anointing, he had submitted to God's timing and had allowed God to be in control. He knew he was God's choice, and the people knew it, too. They were confident that God's Spirit was with David and would guide him and give him success. He was free to take over with authority. How wonderful to have a leader like that! He was teaching his subjects what it meant to follow God.

Seeking Guidance

David sought guidance through prayer. It is significant that the first statement made about David after Saul's death says that he asked God what he should do. "In the course of time, David inquired of the LORD. 'Shall I go up to one of the towns of Judah?' he asked. The LORD said, 'Go up.' David asked, 'Where shall I go?' 'To Hebron,' the LORD answered. So David went" (2 Sam. 2:1, 2). In his fugitive years, David had learned to rely on God and on God's character as he knew it. He knew his God was eager to hear, to answer, and to give him whatever he needed. He also found God ready to impart wisdom. David wanted this to carry over into his role as king. Perhaps he wrote these words in regard to his position:

> I will instruct you and teach you in the way you should
>   go,
> I will counsel you and watch over you . . .
>   the LORD's unfailing love
>   surrounds the man who trusts in him (Ps. 32:8, 10).

As David faced the vacuum left by Saul's death, he was confident God would show him what he was to do next, when he was to do it, and where it was to be done. He did not want to run ahead of God and make wrong decisions and take the wrong paths. Haven't you been in that same spot, wondering what you are to do next or even whether to move at all? We learned about David's reliance on prayer in an emergency situation in 1 Samuel 23, and here again we see him earnestly seeking guidance and wisdom from God to know exactly which way to turn.

God did not disappoint David, just as he never disappoints us. He assured David his idea to go to Judea was a good one, and even specified that he was to settle in Hebron. David might have preferred Bethlehem, his hometown, but he quietly moved his family and his loyal band of men to Hebron, confident that he was moving in harmony with God's will.

When a decision is facing us, like David, we may ask for guidance, and God will help us. We may have to go back to God more than once, and "wait on the Lord" as David did. As we pray, along with reading his Word, he lets us know what path to take. Not that we hear voices or cast lots, but often God leads us through our thoughts, ideas, and desires when we determine to act in accord with Scripture. We can't explain it, but God is faithful to his promise that his Spirit will illuminate our minds so that we have a quiet awareness that we are moving in harmony with him.

If you scan the next few chapters and look for occasions when David prayed, you will see a pattern emerge that must have been his habit, though this is not always recorded. For example, when the safety of the country was threatened in David's first military crisis as king, his first reaction was to turn to God.

Now the Philistines had come and spread out in the Valley of Rephaim; so David inquired of the LORD, "Shall I go and

attack the Philistines? Will you hand them over to me?"
The LORD answered him, "Go, for I will surely hand the
Philistines over to you." So David went to Baal Perazim, and
there he defeated them. He said, "As waters break out, the
LORD has broken out against my enemies before me." . . .
Once more the Philistines came up and spread out in the
Valley of Rephaim; so David inquired of the LORD, and he
answered, "Do not go straight up, but circle behind them
and attack them in front of the balsam trees. As soon as you
hear the sound of marching in the tops of the balsam trees,
move quickly, because that will mean the LORD has gone
out in front of you to strike the Philistine army." So David
did as the LORD commanded him, and he struck down the
Philistines (2 Sam. 5:18–25).

Because David gave prayer top priority, Israel was blessed
in ways that otherwise would never have happened. The
people learned from David that God hears and answers
prayer, that he works for his people by responding to their
prayers. David was careful that prayer had an important
place in his leadership. In your position as a leader have
you seriously adopted and demonstrated a pattern of regular prayer?

Showing Kindness

After David moved to Hebron and the people enthusiastically crowned him king, his first official act was significant. He honored and encouraged the men who had
buried Saul:

He sent messengers to the men of Jabesh Gilead to say to
them, "The LORD bless you for showing this kindness to Saul
your master by burying him. May the LORD now show you
kindness and faithfulness, and I too will show you the same
favor because you have done this. Now then, be strong and

brave, for Saul your master is dead, and the house of Judah has anointed me king over them" (2 Sam. 2:5–7).

David's kindness and compassion must have melted the hearts of Saul's followers and won the admiration of his new subjects. How different this new king was from Saul! David was eager to have a smooth transition of power, and the indications are that he would have been able to win Saul's people over had his own men not been so bloodthirsty and hungry for revenge. A long civil war ensued, which David might have avoided (2 Sam. 3:1).

Another evidence of David's compassion was his desire to show kindness to Saul's descendants. After he was king of all Israel, David went out of his way to discover whether any of Saul's descendants needed help. The king asked, "Is there no one still left of the house of Saul to whom I can show God's kindness?" (2 Sam. 9:3). He located Mephibosheth, Jonathan's son, and found that he had been crippled in an accident as a child at the time of Saul's death (2 Sam. 4:4). David had Ziba, one of Saul's servants, bring Mephibosheth to him:

> The king summoned Ziba, Saul's servant, and said to him, "I have given your master's grandson everything that belonged to Saul and his family. You and your sons and your servants are to farm the land for him and bring in the crops, so that your master's grandson may be provided for. And [he] . . . will always eat at my table" (2 Sam. 9:9, 10).

Mephibosheth was treated like a royal prince. He always ate at the king's table, and David had the joy of knowing he had shown "God's kindness" to Jonathan's son. The word translated "kindness" in this passage is the Hebrew word *hesed,* which is the same word that is often used for mercy and compassion. When Joseph was in prison, we read that "the LORD was with him; he showed him kindness (*hesed*), and granted him favor in the eyes of the prison warden" (Gen. 39:21). Naomi said to her daughters-in-law, "May the LORD show kindness (*hesed*) to you, as you have shown to . . . me" (Ruth 1:8). David had found for himself that God is a God of great mercy; he himself had been the beneficiary of God's *hesed*. Psychologists tell us that we can love only if we know that we are loved. We Christians can truly love, for we know that we are loved by God. David felt surrounded by God's love, and consequently showed great love to others.

As ruler, David had a hard time getting this across to his officials. He got very upset when they did not use kindness and compassion in dealing with their enemies. The episode with Saul's general, Abner, caused David much pain. Abner had been a very loyal and effective general for Saul, admired by friend and foe alike. It reminds us of General Robert E. Lee of the Confederacy. After Saul's death Abner had seen to it that Saul's son Ish-Bosheth was crowned king. Abner's forces, gathered mainly from the tribe of Benjamin, tried to hold out against David, who had a sizable army from the larger tribe of Judah, so a civil war began. "The war between the house of Saul and the house of David lasted a long time. David grew stronger and stronger, while the house of Saul grew weaker and weaker" (2 Sam. 3:1). The tribe of Benjamin, Saul's tribe, was apparently reluctant to give up the material advantages of having one of their members be king (1 Sam. 22:7). But Abner saw it was useless to continue and went to David, surrendered, and pledged him his support. David graciously accepted this gesture, hosted a feast for Abner, whom he respected as an honorable warrior, and together they made a pact "before the LORD" (2 Sam. 5:3).

David expected his officers to follow his lead and welcome Abner as he had done, but the message didn't get through to those rough men. Whether through lack of communication or deliberate willfulness, Joab ambushed and murdered Abner for personal revenge. This grieved David. Instead of praising Joab, he held him responsible and ordered him to mourn Abner's death publicly along with the whole court. David gave Abner a royal burial, while he himself wept aloud at the tomb and fasted, which did not go unnoticed: "All the people took note and were pleased; indeed, everything the king did pleased them. So on that day all the people . . . knew that the king had no part in the murder of Abner" (2 Sam. 3:36, 37).

Leading men to understand his own godly standards was a difficult task for David in those violent times. Referring to Abner, he told his men, "Do you not realize that a prince and a great man has fallen in Israel this day? . . . I am the anointed king . . . these sons of Zeruiah are too strong for me. May the LORD repay the evildoer according to his evil deeds!" (2 Sam. 3:38, 39). Joab and the other sons of Zeruiah, David's half-sister, caused David so much trouble throughout his reign that one wonders if David should have been more severe in his discipline of Joab at this point. There is evidence that one of David's weaknesses may have been his hesitancy to discipline, as we will see later in his dealings with his own children. All he did in this case was to prophesy an evil end for Joab, which came true much later (1 Kings 2:28–35), but was that long-delayed sentence severe enough for cold-blooded murder? Overzealous loyalty is difficult to deal with, and the barbaric methods and cruelty of these men sickened David. Many a leader and many a parent has agonized over the problems of how harshly to discipline and what the consequences will be if they are either too hard or too soft.

David was appalled when two of Saul's former soldiers murdered Ish-Bosheth, Saul's son. David might well have won the prince over without any bloodshed, as he had done with Abner. Evidently the men saw this as a chance to ingratiate themselves with David, the new king. If so, they were in for a rude surprise, for instead of praise, David said to them:

> "When a man told me, 'Saul is dead,' and thought he was
> bringing me good news, I seized him and put him to death.
> . . . How much more—when wicked men have killed an
> innocent man in his own house and on his own bed—
> should I not now demand his blood from your hand and
> rid the earth of you!" (2 Sam. 4:10, 11).

He then exerted his authority and ordered capital punishment for them, and honored Ish-Bosheth with a burial in Abner's tomb. David was a strong king, but he was also compassionate, ruling with *hesed,* the kindness and mercy he had learned from God. Perhaps that, as much as anything else, won the people's allegiance, and he was able to unify and solidify the nation.

> All the tribes came to David at Hebron and said, "We are
> your own flesh and blood. In the past, while Saul was king
> over us, you were the one who led Israel on their military
> campaigns. And the LORD said to you, 'You will shepherd
> my people Israel, and you will become their ruler.'" When
> all the elders of Israel had come to King David at Hebron,
> the king made a compact with them at Hebron before the
> LORD, and they anointed David king over Israel (2 Sam.
> 5:1–4).

Successful Administration

David led with skill administratively and militarily. It is hard for us to grasp what an enormous task lay before David. When he took over, Israel was surrounded by powerful adversaries. On every border strong enemies were ready to pounce on the little country, to swallow her up, squeeze her out, or just to infiltrate and weaken from within. Within Israel itself there were deep divisions after the long civil war. Abner and Saul's son had both been killed by David's men. There were different factions, divided loyalties, and old wounds that needed to be healed before a strong kingdom could be built. It was an enormous task that would take strong leadership, but it was David's job to do. Those first years of David's reign were summed up in this line: "The LORD gave David victory everywhere he went" (2 Sam. 8:14). God had called him to fill the role of king, and he would help him do it well.

In the New Testament, one of the key verses to understanding Paul's life is, "Thanks be unto God, who always leads us in triumphal procession in Christ" (2 Cor. 2:14). To Paul, whether he was speaking to the intellectuals of Athens, visiting remote villages, or lying in chains in a jail cell in Rome, he was convinced God meant to make him triumph for the sake of the gospel. To David, whether he was in an isolated cave leading a group of malcontents, or serving as a popular, revered king of Israel, he was confident that God meant for him to succeed. He knew God had plans that only he could carry out, and he counted on God to give him whatever help he needed.

Suppose you have a Sunday school class of ten or twelve teenagers, and you are the only teacher those young people will have in a given year. In that assignment, God means for you to do well, not just slide through. Do you try to get to know each member of the class? Do you research the best way to go about teaching them and reaching them with God's truths? Do you pray for them individually? Apply this kind of approach to all the places of responsibility you have, and then ask God to fill in the gaps in your abilities and give you the time to make you to triumph "in Christ who through us spreads everywhere the fragrance of the knowledge of him. For we are to God the aroma of Christ among those who are being saved" (2 Cor. 2:14, 15).

Over the next few years David excelled in military conquest, in administration, and in personal relationships. The biblical account is very modest, but historians tell us that it was astounding what David accomplished. Not only did he push the enemies back on all borders, but he gained a buffer zone as well. The Hittites were humbled, the Philistines were driven to a tiny strip of land along the Mediterranean, and the king of Tyre wanted to be David's ally. Jerusalem was established as a strong capital city, highways were opened, commerce and trade flourished, and Israel became one of the strongest powers in the Middle East. The size of the country increased from about six thousand square miles to sixty thousand square miles.

David's skillful leadership was vital. He was highly respected and acclaimed, but he wanted the people to give the credit to God. He wanted them to know it was in answer to prayer and through God's love for them that they were becoming a strong nation. To assure that this message was clear, David gave top priority to revitalizing the religious life of Israel.

Spiritual Interest Restored

David restored joyous worship to Israel. He revived an intense interest in spiritual things. He set high standards for the tabernacle services. When the ark of the covenant was brought to Jerusalem (2 Sam. 6), a whole new religious era was ushered in. Many more priests were needed. Hundreds of musicians were trained, songs were sung, and instruments played (v. 5). "That day David first committed to Asaph and his associates this psalm of thanks to the LORD" (1 Chron. 16:7). This was when hymns of praise were first introduced into Israel's public worship. Soon after, the pattern of responsive singing by antiphonal choirs was instituted. This is part of the song David composed for the celebration when the ark was brought to Jerusalem:

Give thanks to the LORD, call on his name;
    make known among the nations what he has done.

Sing to him, sing praise to him;
  tell of all his wonderful acts;
Glory to his holy name;
  let the hearts of those who seek the LORD rejoice.
Look to the LORD and his strength;
  seek his face always (Ps. 105:1–4).

David in many ways exemplified what a leader should be. He accepted God's calling him to his position and sought the Lord's guidance in all things. He searched the law of the Lord to establish his moral standards. He understood that he was not to "lord it over" his people, but rather to be their kind servant. He gave priority to restoring joy and praise to their lives and their religion. By letting God use him as his servant, he was successful in leading his kingdom to new heights. Like Canada geese flying in formation, Israel was able to advance further under his leadership than anyone dreamed possible.

What a joy for David to guide the people into praise for the majesty and greatness of God! What a joy it is for us when God allows us to fill leadership roles and uses us to guide others into appreciation and praise for his unfathomable character—for his love, his wisdom, his power, and his majesty.

2

God Reassures David, the Grateful Subject

Primary Scripture Reading

2 Samuel 7
1 Chronicles 28

Supplementary References

Exodus 25:10–22
Psalm 24, 90, 103, 145, 119:89
Zephaniah 3:20
2 Chronicles 6:1–17
Romans 11:33

Questions for Study and Discussion

1. How do you picture life in Jerusalem to be at this time (2 Sam. 5:6–12, 1 Chron. 15:1, and 1 Chron. 6:31–32, 48–49)?

How did David describe his lifestyle in 2 Samuel 7?

Does your lifestyle sometimes bother you when you see the needs of God's people?

What were David's priorities?

What were his motives? (Support your answer).

2. What was the significance of the ark of the covenant (Exod. 25:10–22)?

   What activities had David instituted to make the ark meaningful to the people (1 Chron. 15:16; 16:4–6)?

3. What encouragement did David get for his plan (2 Sam. 7)?

   What did David's relationship with Nathan seem to be?

   What rating would you give Nathan as David's spiritual advisor?

   Describe what you think was Nathan's role in David's life as king.

4. Why did God review his past instructions about the ark?

   What was God's relationship to the ark?

   What effect would this review have on David?

   Why did God remind David of his past?

   List the steps through which God guided David's thinking as he refused his request. Does God ever take you through these same steps?

5. Notice the promises God gave David. Fill in the chart below showing which were for David, for Israel, and for us.

David	The Nation Israel	All Believers

6. After hearing God's words for him, was David disappointed in not building the temple?

What promise about the future temple did God give him that brought joy to David?

About Israel?

What role did God give David in the building of the temple (1 Chron. 28)?

7. How did David now see himself (2 Sam. 7)?

How did he see God?

What was it about God that so amazed him?

Can you recall a time when you had a refusal from God, but the goodness of his plans turned out to far exceed yours?

Reword David's prayer to fit your situation, expressing your own love, gratitude, and petitions.

*N*one of us likes to be told no, especially when we think we have a wonderful idea. David thought he had a great idea, but God said No, and David's reaction gives a glimpse of how David could tune his heart to God's heart. Even though God rejected David's request to build the temple, his gentle no brought a deep expression of love and exultation from David. He was overcome with gratitude both for God's greatness and for God's personal concern for him. The encounter between David and God highlights some of the secrets of their special relationship. Examining this passage in detail enables us to see both the heart of David and the heart of God.

A Resolve to Build God a House

> After the king was settled in his palace and the LORD had given him rest from all his enemies around him, he said to Nathan the prophet, "Here I am, living in a palace of cedar, while the ark of God remains in a tent." Nathan replied to the king, "Whatever you have in mind, go ahead and do it, for the LORD is with you" (2 Sam. 7:1–3).

Can you see what David was thinking? He was now living in a beautiful palace, built with magnificent materials sent by the king of Tyre; he had all that he needed for his comfort and pleasure. His country was at peace, many buildings were being constructed in Jerusalem (1 Chron. 15:1), and most of the people were living in houses. The ark of the covenant had been brought to Jerusalem with great celebration and rejoicing, but there was no suitable place to keep it. Worship services were flourishing and large numbers of people came to gather around the ark for singing, for playing instruments, and for the sacrifices. Is it any wonder David felt the need for a beautiful building in which to house the ark? Wouldn't that show honor and reverence for God, and show that this was the most important aspect of Israel's life? You can almost hear David saying to himself, "Where are your priorities?" David was king over Israel, but to him God was the true king.

We cannot begin to understand David's desire to build a temple unless we understand the significance of the ark in Israel's history. When God called his people out of Egypt, and Moses led them to Canaan, God demonstrated his power and protection in countless ways. When Pharaoh and his armies were pursuing the Israelites and had almost caught up with them, God directed Moses and Aaron to strike the Red Sea with a rod. To the Israelites' joyful astonishment they saw the waters part, and walked across dry sand to safety. God manifested his presence with Israel in the form of a cloud by day and a pillar of fire by night. He fed them with manna and quail in the desert, and provided water from a rock Moses struck with a rod, all vividly recounted in Exodus 14–18. After three months of traveling, they came to Mount Sinai, and there God met with Moses in a most unusual way, a meeting that was to change the history of Israel. First of all, he pledged himself to them as his people.

> Then Moses went up to God, and the LORD called to him from the mountain and said, "This is what you are to say to the house of Jacob and what you are to tell the people of Israel: 'You yourselves have seen what I did to Egypt, and how I carried you on eagles' wings and brought you to myself. Now if you obey me fully and keep my covenant, then out of all nations you will be my treasured possession. Although the whole earth is mine, you will be for me a kingdom of priests and a holy nation.' These are the words you are to speak to the Israelites" (Exod. 19:3–6).

It was at that time that God gave Moses the Ten Commandments, and many other specific instructions about how his people were to conduct themselves, and about their responsibilities to him and to each other. God also revealed to Moses his plans for a tabernacle, a word meaning dwelling place. Israel was to build it to God's exact specifications which he proceeded to give to Moses: "Have them build a sanctuary for me, and I will dwell among them. Make this tabernacle and all its furnishings exactly like the pattern I will show you" (Exod. 25:8). God wanted the people to know that along with his power (his omnipotence), and his wisdom, given in carefully stated words to them (his omniscience), they also had his assurance that he was always present with them (his omnipresence). He wanted them to be aware constantly that he intended to keep his promises given to Abraham and the other patriarchs. God gave Moses detailed instructions, and the tabernacle was indeed built according to God's divine plan. It was placed in the very center of the camp, so that it would be seen continually by the people and they would be reminded of God's faithfulness.

The ark of the covenant, described fully in Exodus 25:10–24, was the central focus of the tabernacle, and was also at the very heart of Jewish religious life. It was a box overlaid with gold, in which were placed the Ten Commandments, "the gold jar of manna," and "Aaron's staff that had budded" (Heb. 9:4). Its cover, called the mercy seat or the atonement cover, was of great significance, for it was the site of God's act of grace in accepting atonement for sin and forgiving and reconciling his people. The ark was the most sacred piece of temple furniture, and was kept in the Holy of Holies, where only the High Priest was allowed to go once a year on the Day of Atonement. On that day he took the blood from the sin offering, sprinkled it on the lid of the ark, and on behalf of the people, confessed their sin, and asked forgiveness for them. This ceremony was extremely important because God was teaching them about redemption through blood sacrifice, which pointed to the one perfect sacrifice, the perfect Lamb of God, even Jesus Christ.

It seems that throughout Saul's reign the ark was ignored except when Saul almost superstitiously hoped that taking it with him to battle would somehow bring God's protection and victory (1 Sam. 14:18). David, however, understood both the symbol and the reality of God's mercy, and he wanted it restored to its former place in Israel's religious life and worship. It is not hard to see why he would want it placed in a beautiful, more permanent structure.

Things may have been a bit quiet for David at that time, with nothing too pressing on his calendar, for there was remarkable unity, stability, and prosperity in the country. The military battles recorded in chapters 8 and 9 probably took place sometime after the events of chapter 5, and the accounts dealing with the ark were put together topically rather than in chronological order.

We hear today a lot about the different management styles of our leaders. Some executives are aloof from the daily events and delegate a great deal to others, while other leaders involve themselves with the details of the job and try to stay abreast of everything. David's management style must have been excellent, for things were running extremely well, except, as David viewed it, the religious part of their national life. A tent was a good place for the ark when the Israelites were moving about, but now they had a capital city with buildings and houses, and David longed for God's dwelling place to once again be the central focus, the most prominent structure of all, which would be seen from every vantage point possible, and be a reminder to the people of God's preeminence in their national life, and of his faithfulness to them. Wasn't it only right that God have a magnificent temple? He should have the best house of all!

It is interesting that David spoke with Nathan, the prophet, about his plan, counting on him to help him find God's will. We have to admire David for doing this rather than going off on his own, but one wonders about Nathan's answer to David. He responded quickly and glibly that God would be with David all the way and encouraged him in effect to "go for it!" Nathan seemed as enamored with the idea as David. Probably he was very impressed with David, certainly the best king he had ever seen and a man of great faith. However, as a spiritual advisor to a king, surely Nathan should have consulted with God on such an ambitious undertaking and sought his guidance. Is this not a reminder to us to be careful to consult with God before we glibly give out advice and counsel? It is easy to be swept along with apparently wonderful schemes, and we often forget to pray and seek God's wisdom in the matter.

A Request Refused

"That night the word of the LORD came to Nathan, saying, 'Go and tell my servant David, "This is what the Lord says"'" (2 Sam. 7:4, 5). Then God, gently but firmly, in terms that would not be misunderstood, gave Nathan his instructions for David. David was not to be the one to build the temple. In one of the most tender passages in the Bible, God carefully explained that he must say no to David. Years later, when David was giving the plans of the temple to Solomon, he recounted that God had said, "You are not to build a house for my Name, because you are a warrior and have shed blood" (1 Chron. 28:3). His house was to be built in a time of peace by David's son, not when there was still fighting for territory and security. God had called David to be, among other things, a brilliant general who could lead in battles and could inspire his men to fight for Israel and make her secure from her enemies. David showed that he understood his role and accepted it.

A Reminder of Relationships

When Nathan came the next day with the message from God, David was deeply moved by God's words for him, which included reminders of some very important things about their relationship.

First of all, God let David know that there was nothing wrong with his proposal to build him a house, but that God had a different timetable. This must have impressed David, because he told his son Solomon about it. Some thirty years later when Solomon dedicated the finished temple, he said to the people, "The LORD said to my father David . . . 'You did well to have this in your heart. Nevertheless, you are not the one to build the temple, but your son'" (2 Chron. 6:8–9). Without scolding David or putting him down for his suggestion, God took David into his thinking and his plans, and showed David his perspective:

> Go and tell my servant David, "This is what the LORD says: Are you the one to build me a house to dwell in? I have not dwelt in a house from the day I brought the Israelites up out of Egypt to this day. I have been moving from place to place with a tent as my dwelling. Wherever I have moved with all the Israelites, did I ever say to any of their rulers whom I commanded to shepherd my people Israel, 'Why have you not built me a house of cedar?'" (2 Sam. 7:5–7).

God began by pointing out that the house was David's idea, not his, and that he had never told anyone to build a permanent structure for him. The tabernacle was moved from place to place with the Israelites, and this was important, for it signified his constant presence with them. He reminded David that in their relationship he, God, was the one in charge. David knew that the tabernacle and all of its symbolism had been designed by God. Every detail had been specified, because every detail had meaning. Furthermore, in the New Testament we find it meant even more, for it illustrated Christ and God's plan of redemption (see Heb. 8–11). God firmly told David that it was God's prerogative and his alone to make any changes if they were to be made (vv. 5–7), and that he had never instructed any of the shepherds whom he had called to lead Israel to build a house.

I am sure David was listening intently to this strong language from God about the ark of the covenant, because he had already made one colossal blunder when transporting it (2 Sam. 6). The ark was to be carried in a carefully prescribed manner, and because that procedure was not followed, tragedy had occurred. David knew God meant what he said. Sometimes it is hard for us to let God be God, especially when he says no to one of our good ideas. At such times we need to stop and reflect again on our relationship with him, and remember who he is—the sovereign Lord.

A Review of David's Past, Present, and Future

In 2 Samuel 7:8–11 God describes David's past, present, and future. He reminds David of who he (David) is. Before David ever shepherded Israel, he was just tending sheep back in Judea. "This is what the LORD Almighty says: I took you from the pasture and from following the flock to be ruler over my people Israel. I have been with you wherever you have gone, and I have cut off all your enemies from before you" (vv. 8, 9). You were a follower, David, and I have made you a leader! God saw that David was thoroughly humbled by then, for God's tone changed. What the sovereign Lord revealed then astounded David, for he shared with David his purposes for David's and Israel's future:

> Now I will make your name great, like the names of the greatest men of the earth. And I will provide a place for my people Israel and will plant them so that they can have a

home of their own and no longer be disturbed. . . . I will also give you rest from all your enemies (vv. 9–11).

David's name was well known in his day, but is there any one human being throughout the centuries whose name is better known than David's? When I stood and marveled at Michelangelo's sculpture of David in Florence, I wasn't prepared for the emotional experience it brought. Many people have a similar reaction, especially those who have appreciated David through the Bible. Not only because the sculpture is superbly done, but because of what David's life and his psalms have meant to them.

God then proceeds to reveal his plans for Israel: to provide for them a home where there is peace, security, and rest from their enemies. God restated this promise to his people through the years, as to Zephaniah, the prophet:

> At that time I will gather you;
> at that time I will bring you home.
> I will give you honor and praise
> among all the peoples of the earth
> when I restore your fortunes
> before your very eyes (Zeph. 3:20).

A Redirection in Thinking

God's next words to David are moving. David had wanted to build God a house, and now God said, "The LORD himself will establish a house for you." What a loving thing for God to say to David! He assured David that, when he died, his offspring would be king, and the temple David longed to build would indeed be constructed by David's own son. Then God added, "My love will never be taken away from him." Wouldn't those be wonderful words for a father to hear? We all worry about what may happen to our children in the future. God concludes with this staggering promise: "Your house and your kingdom will endure forever." What could God mean by that?

Reverence for God as God

David listened with rapt attention while Nathan was giving him these words from God, and when he had finished, David wanted to be alone with God. "Then King David went in and sat before the LORD" (2 Sam. 7:18). David was overwhelmed. It was hard for him to take this all in. He caught from God the glory of what he was saying. David's own son would be king and would have the privilege of building the temple, and his kingdom would go on forever! We know now that God was looking way past David and Solomon right down to Christ and to the spiritual kingdom that he would establish, truths that extended far beyond what David could take in. But David again gained new knowledge of what God is and shows by his words of praise his concept of God's character, and his appreciation for "the heart of God."

1. A personal, communicating God. David was overcome by God's mercy. It made him see himself for what he was, and he cried out, "Who am I, O Sovereign LORD, and what is my family, that you have brought me so far?" (2 Sam. 7:18). Don't you often ponder the same question? God had brought David far beyond his expectations and, as he thought back on all God had done, he saw his own insignificance. He felt his smallness, and it suddenly dawned on him that the eternal God, the sovereign Lord, was sharing with him, a mere man, his plans and purposes for the future.

O Sovereign LORD, you have also spoken about the future of the house of your servant. Is this your usual way of dealing with man, O Sovereign LORD? What more can David say to you? For you know your servant, O Sovereign LORD. For the sake of your word and according to your will, you have done this great thing and made it known to your servant (2 Sam. 7:19, 20).

David was speechless! How unusual for David; he couldn't find words to express his feelings. To think that God would share his thoughts with him, a nobody from an insignificant family!

The fact that God communicates with us mere human beings is awesome, and for some it is hard to believe. God has spoken in a very direct way to us through the Bible. The disciples had Jesus Christ in person to "show them the Father"; the Old Testament saints had direct revelations that were unmistakably from God. We today have the privilege of having in our hands the written revelation from both of these eras to read, to study, and to meditate on. The New Testament is there so we may absorb its truths about Christ: his life, his death, and his resurrection. As we read and study, the Bible becomes a living book, carrying its own sense of authority. God is communicating to us so that we are drawn to see the majesty and grace of Christ, and we are humbled, even as David was. We are overwhelmed that God is speaking to us! We, too, are awed by this marvelous truth about his character: he is great and he is personal.

> Your word, O LORD, is eternal;
>   it stands firm in the heavens.
> Your faithfulness continues through all generations;
>   you established the earth, and it endures.
> How sweet are your promises to my taste,
>   sweeter than honey to my mouth! (Ps. 119:89, 90, 103).

2. A great and mighty God. God was very personal to David, and then it suddenly seemed incomprehensible to him that a God so personal could also be so great and majestic. He broke out in praise, "How great you are, O Sovereign LORD!" (2 Sam. 7:22). David was filled with awe and wonder, and he was deeply grateful. In Psalm 145 he expressed how he felt about God, that he is both great and personal:

> Great is the LORD and most worthy of praise;
>   his greatness no one can fathom.
> One generation will commend your works to another;
>   they will tell of your mighty acts.
> They will speak of the glorious splendor of your majesty
>   and I will meditate on your wonderful works
>   (Ps. 145:3–5).

> The LORD is righteous in all his ways
>   and loving toward all he has made.
> The LORD is near to all who call on him,
>   to all who call on him in truth.
> He fulfills the desires of those who fear him;
>   he hears their cry and saves them
>   (Ps. 145:17–19).

3. A trustworthy God. David saw clearly that God was the only true God. "There is no one like you, and there is no God but you" (2 Sam. 7:22). God never disappoints us as other gods do. If our gods are materialism, fame, money, or pleasure, they will not ultimately satisfy. They never come through with promised rewards. Only Jehovah God is totally reliable and completely true. "Oh, the depth of the riches of the wisdom and knowledge of God! How unsearchable his judgments, and his paths beyond tracing out!" (Rom. 11:33).

4. An everlasting God. How grateful David was when he thought of all that God planned to do for Israel. God had already done so much, and now to think of the future God described warmed David's heart with love. God had delivered them from Egypt, had driven their enemies out of

Canaan, and had established them in the land and in Jerusalem; in fact, God promised they were "established forever."

I imagine that by now David had fallen to his knees in adoration. He was grateful for all that God had revealed to him, and he responded with a prayer.

> O Sovereign LORD, you are God! Your words are trustworthy, and you have given this good promise to your servant. Now be pleased to bless the house of your servant, that it may continue forever in your sight; for you, O Sovereign LORD, have spoken, and with your blessing the house of your servant will be blessed forever (2 Sam. 7:28–29).

David was able to have an important role in the answer to that prayer. This was not the end of the story for David in regard to the temple. God gave to him the plans for the temple and gave him the privilege of collecting all of the materials so that when Solomon began the construction, the plans and materials were ready to the last detail. Before he died, he turned all of these over to Solomon. We read, "He gave him the plans of all that the Spirit had put in his mind. . . . 'All this is in writing . . . because the hand of the LORD was upon me, and he gave me understanding in all the details of the plan'" (1 Chron. 28:12, 19). He led the people in praise at that time, then was overwhelmed once again by the greatness of God and his own insignificance. He considered it a blessing and a privilege to even be allowed to contribute to the temple. "Who am I, and who are my people, that we should be able to give as generously as this? Everything comes from you, and we have given you only what comes from your hand" (1 Chron. 29:14).

God said no to David's request to build the temple; instead he said, "I will build a house for you." David offered to do something for God; instead, God showed his majesty and what he planned to do for David. David proposed an earthly structure; instead, God promised a never-ending kingdom that could be seen only by faith. This promise was gloriously fulfilled in David's descendant Jesus Christ, our everlasting king.

These words have inspired praise through the centuries, a fulfillment of David's heart's desire that God be honored as he deserves:

> Lift up your heads, O you gates,
>   be lifted up, you ancient doors,
>   that the King of glory may come in.
> Who is this King of glory?
>   the LORD strong and mighty,
>   the LORD mighty in battle. . . .
> Who is he, this King of glory?
>   the LORD Almighty—
>   he is the King of glory (Ps. 24:7, 8, 10).

3

God Convicts David, the Royal Adulterer

Primary Scripture Reading

2 Samuel 11

Supplementary References

Exodus 20:1–17
Deuteronomy
17:16–20
Leviticus 20:10
2 Corinthians
10:4, 5
Colossians 3:5–10

Questions for Study and Discussion

1. Read 2 Samuel 11. In verse 1 do you find some hints that David may have been particularly vulnerable to temptation at this time? (For background, read 2 Sam. 10:17–19; Deut. 17:16–20; 2 Sam. 3:1–5 and 5:13–16.)

2. Using the rest of the chapter and the headings below, chart the series of steps David took that led him ever deeper into sin.

Verse(s)	Temptation	Actions/Choices	Whom it Affected

3. What alternatives do you think were available to David at each step in the above chart?

4. Try to put yourself in David's place. How was he probably rationalizing and excusing his sin?

   Read Exodus 20:1–17. Which of the Ten Commandments did David break?

5. Read Paul's list of pitfalls for the Christian in Colossians 3:5–10. To which do you find yourself most vulnerable?

   Identify subtle thoughts that sometimes come to your mind and will lead to sin if you allow them to take root. What has helped you to stop the process once you recognized it?

   What were the results when you failed to take action to stop the downward progression?

6. Was Bathsheba blameless?

   What percentage of blame would you assign to her and to David?

   Read 2 Samuel 13:12, 13. Why, in your opinion, did Bathsheba not use arguments similar to Tamar's to help David realize what he was doing?

   Review 1 Samuel 25. Compare David's encounters with Abigail and Bathsheba as to David's actions, the women's actions, and God's actions.

7. 2 Samuel 11:26, 27 is a very brief summary covering several months. From what you have learned in previous passages about David's desires, purposes, and the guiding principles in his life, what, do you think, was happening in his heart during those months that is not recorded here?

*I*t was a balmy spring evening in Jerusalem. Perhaps it was very warm inside the palace, for David could not sleep. He "got up from his bed and walked around on the roof of the palace" (2 Samuel 11:2). David's palace roof probably stood higher than most of the nearby houses and was more like a penthouse garden than a plain, flat roof, large enough to walk around in privacy and look over the lovely city. What satisfaction it gave him to know that he had conquered this fortress from the Jebusites (2 Sam. 5:6–9) and had built it into his capital city, using the beautiful pinkish-white stone native to the area. The sun had set, and a cool desert breeze brought welcome relief from the heat of the day. Myriads of stars twinkled in the clear desert sky. David could have written some of his psalms from that roof, lines such as "When I consider your heavens, the work of your fingers, the moon and the stars, which you have set in place, what is man that you are mindful of him, the son of man that you care for him?" (Ps. 8:3, 4). Perhaps he remembered that God had promised Abraham that his descendants would be as numerous as the stars in the sky.

On this particular night, David was no doubt wondering how his troops were faring. Why hadn't he heard from them? He thought about the previous year's great victories over the Arameans and the retreat of the Ammonites. The

Ammonites had fallen back into their walled cities, and this spring's campaign would complete the mopping-up process. It seemed anticlimactic for David to go again. Maybe he should have gone, but it was much more comfortable being in the palace than marching and camping out in the open, so "David sent Joab out with the king's men and the whole Israelite army. They destroyed the Ammonites and besieged Rabbah. But David remained in Jerusalem" (2 Sam. 11:1). Joab was a good commander, but he worried David at times. He wouldn't get into anything he couldn't handle, or would he? His amoral standards were often appalling. David was very likely mulling over some of these things.

As he paced back and forth on the roof, David could catch glimpses of families in their homes, and wondered what his own wives and children were doing. Were his wives putting their children to bed? He loved to watch his children. He was proud of them. Why hadn't he spent more time with them? Where had the years gone? Why couldn't a king have a more normal life? He felt very lonely at times.

Decision to Sin

Suddenly his eyes fell on a woman bathing. Most likely she was unaware that anyone was watching, she took her time, and David did not look away. Her appearance delighted him. She was beautiful! Who was she? David had to find out. Thoughts of Joab, his army, and his own wives and children were forgotten; he called to a servant to find out about her. The man reported, "Isn't this Bathsheba, the daughter of Eliam and the wife of Uriah the Hittite?" (2 Sam. 11:2, 3).

This information should have flashed a red warning signal to David. Both Uriah and Eliam were included among David's "mighty men" listed in 2 Samuel 23, brave warriors who had been chosen to serve in the royal guard. They had probably declared their loyalty to David early in his fugitive years when he badly needed support. David could have known them personally, and he surely knew what a noble man Uriah was. Perhaps in that culture a king could call for a beautiful girl and add her to his harem, but when David found out Bathsheba was Uriah's wife, that should have been the end of it. What David did next was clearly wrong and led to violation of God's commands (Lev. 18:20). To admire her beauty was one thing, but the events that follow are so far from what we expect from David that we can hardly believe what we are reading. We are shocked that he would fall into actions so contrary to his nature. We are shocked, that is, unless we understand the nature of sin and the way it takes control when we fail to curb temptations at the outset, while they are still only in our thoughts. This chapter reminds us to be alert and heed the warnings of trouble ahead.

Deliberate First Step

When David gave the order to have Bathsheba brought to the palace, he took the first in a series of deliberate overt steps. He made a decision to follow his inclinations in spite of Bathsheba's marital status, in spite of his relationship with Uriah, and in spite of his knowledge of God's clear standards for him. In effect, he said to himself, "I see something I want, and I'm going to have it, no matter whom it hurts."

Isn't our first step into sin often the same as David's? Had David's conscience been as keen as it once was, he would have stopped at one of several points and said to himself, "Hey, this is all wrong!" He might have gone so far as to have a lovely dinner party with Bathsheba, and then no matter what her attraction, cried out to God for help: "Lord, bring me to my senses, and give me the strength to send Uriah's wife home." He had sought God's help many times in the past when faced with more obvious enemies, but perhaps he rationalized and thought to himself: "I'm the king. I've risked my life over and over for these people. Don't kings have the power and right to take what they want?" David made his decision and slept with Bathsheba.

David evidently expected this to be a one-night affair, known to only a few trusted servants, that would soon be forgotten. He was in for a rude awakening, however, when word came from Bathsheba that she was pregnant. No wonder movies have been made about this story, and books have been written about it. It has all the sensational elements: a luxurious setting, beautiful, famous people, drama, intrigue, sex, violence. It's all there, and even a Watergate-type cover-up (or should we call it Bathwatergate?).

Deception Begins

David was now in a quandary. What was he to do? Looking back, we can see several things he might have done. He could have called Uriah home, admitted his selfishness and indiscretion to Uriah, to Bathsheba, and to God, and humbly asked for forgiveness. Some solution could have been worked out with the least hurt all around. But no, David's first thought was self-preservation, and he did just what we are prone to do: He made plans to cover his tracks. Look at his next steps:

So David sent word to Joab: "Send me Uriah the Hittite." And Joab sent him to David. When Uriah came to him . . . David said to Uriah, "Go down to your house and wash your feet." So Uriah left the palace, and a gift from the king was sent after him. But Uriah slept at the entrance to the palace with all his master's servants and did not go down to his house (2 Sam. 11:6–9).

Now what? The cover-up was not working. David was sure that if Uriah came home, he would be eager to be with his beautiful wife, and no one would ever know that David was the father of the child, least of all Uriah. But when Uriah came home, he was too noble a soldier to fall in with David's scheme. He felt it only right and honorable that he sleep with the "master's servants" at the gate of the palace instead of accepting the special privilege of going home to be with his wife. Now David had to devise a new plan to deceive Uriah and continue the cover-up:

> When David was told, "Uriah did not go home," he asked him, "Haven't you just come from a distance? Why didn't you go home?" Uriah said to David, "The ark and Israel and Judah are staying in tents, and my master Joab and my lord's men are camped in the open fields. How could I go to my house and eat and drink and lie with my wife? As surely as I live, I will not do such a thing!" . . . At David's invitation he ate and drank with him, and David made him drunk. But in the evening Uriah went out to sleep on his mat among his master's servants; he did not go home (2 Sam. 11:10–14).

Imagine David's being such a hypocrite as to show Uriah all that unusual favor and kindness. He urged him to go home, gave him two more days' leave, invited him to a dinner party, and then got him drunk so that his sense of duty would be dulled and he would go home to be with his wife. Does this sound like David, who was always so open, honest, and anything but devious?

Death Decreed

Uriah's actions and responses must have pierced David's heart like a knife. David now felt trapped, and the only way out seemed to be to get rid of Uriah:

In the morning David wrote a letter to Joab and sent it
with Uriah. In it he wrote, "Put Uriah in the front line where
the fighting is fiercest. Then withdraw from him so he will
be struck down and die." So while Joab had the city under
siege he put Uriah at a place where he knew the strongest
defenders were. When the men of the city came out and
fought against Joab, some of the men in David's army fell;
moreover Uriah the Hittite was dead (2 Sam. 11:14–17).

How horrible to deliberately plan Uriah's death and then
have Uriah himself deliver the message that arranged it
while he would be fighting bravely for the king who had
seemed to treat him so royally! When the messenger came
back to David with the news that Uriah had died along
with quite a few other soldiers, how crass David was! His
reply was false and flippant, designed not to give away his
role. In our vernacular it amounted to, "Well, that's the
way the cookie crumbles in battles. You win some and you
lose some. Tell Joab not to worry about it." How callous
and self-righteous! This was so unlike David, we wonder
why the words didn't stick in his throat. We can almost
predict the regret and remorse that lay ahead for him. For
one whose life was "bound in the bundle of life with the
LORD," as Abigail had put it many years before (1 Sam. 25:29
KJV), this attitude could not continue indefinitely.

Consider this event from Joab's perspective. He, like the
other soldiers, greatly admired David. David had raised the
sights of those men when they joined him and helped him
evade the cruel Saul. David had avoided the tricky, con-
niving methods of men of lower standards. It was a new
experience for those rough men to have a leader who knew
God and consulted him before making decisions. What
could David teach Joab now? David's true reason for the
strange orders about Uriah may not have been clear to Joab
at first, but you can be sure that when he got home he put
two and two together. To take him into this scheme placed

David in a very vulnerable spot with respect to Joab. To have Joab think David operated on the same level as he did, with intrigue, secret reprisals and hidden motives, weakened David's authority as Joab's superior from then on, and may account for Joab's later arrogance and willfulness in the face of David's plans and orders.

Derived Benefits

In a way, it is sad that this raw nerve in David's life had to be exposed. Wouldn't it have been better if the writers of the Bible had just left out this event? Couldn't they have said, "Uriah was killed in battle and David took his widow to be his wife"? Many times the Bible encapsulates periods of time in a few verses, so why not here?

There are several reasons we should be deeply grateful this entire story is included in the Bible. For one thing, it is hard for some of us to identify with the great men and women of the Bible. When we read of these outstanding individuals, we often consider them so far above us that we could never attain to their spirituality or their great deeds. David was not perfect. He lied to Ahimelech (1 Sam. 21), and it cost the priest his life, as well as the lives of many other innocent people. His anger at Nabal and his desire for revenge were so strong he would have killed him and all of his servants had Abigail not stopped him (1 Sam. 25). David learned from these sins; he allowed God to convict, mold, and teach him. We, too, learn from them. We find throughout the pages of Scripture that men like Moses, Abraham, Hezekiah, and even the great prophet Elijah had failures that are set down for our benefit. The fact that the Bible draws aside the curtain and allows us to enter into David's vulnerability and failure binds us to him in a way his successes alone never could.

Another reason it is important this story was recorded is that it attests to the truth of Scripture. Writers from other ancient cultures were careful to omit anything unflattering about their heroes, but God's Word does not hold up false expectations that we could never reach. The men God used as his leaders were human beings with the same weaknesses and frailties we have. The Holy Spirit guided the writers of the Bible to write the truth about their blemishes and flaws so that we can learn from their mistakes, and also to show us how God used them in amazing ways in spite of their weaknesses. God's dealing with men and women when they fail shows us facets of his character that we need to grasp when we fail him. The way the Bible presents the true nature of man and the true nature of God speaks for its validity and inspiration.

We are also thankful for what this story shows us about our own natures and tendencies to sin. Outwardly sinful behavior such as David's erupted from something wrong deep inside. It is interesting that of the Ten Commandments, the first four deal with our relationship with God, the next five with our relationships with others, and the last speaks to what goes on inside the heart. The tenth commandment states, "You shall not covet . . . anything that belongs to your neighbor" (Exod. 20:17). We are not to covet his lifestyle, his house, his wife, his mode of transportation, be it an oxcart or a shiny new car, or anything that someone else has. Think about how many of our sins and failures have their roots in coveting. Someone has said, "Sin is demanding what God has not chosen to give." David lusted for someone God had not chosen to give him, and it created a lot of problems for him and many other people. Each new problem called for another decision. As the number of bad choices mounted, each required a new cover-up. Finally, David became tangled in a web of sin that was too much for him to unravel. While we may not have exactly the same temptations David had, our desires to covet what God has not chosen to give us can also lead us into a series of unintended and painful situations.

Downward Steps

Let's review the steps David took, and look at the way the New Testament recognizes the same problems and gives practical help:

1. *He let impure thoughts and desires linger and grow in his mind.* Paul recognized this danger and often wrote about our inner warfare and struggles with sin, which begin in our minds. He emphasized the fact that our spiritual weapons are "mighty through God" (KJV), can demolish even our sinful imaginations, and "take captive every thought to make it obedient to Christ" (2 Cor. 10:4, 5). Paul also provided us with both a warning and a promise regarding our struggles with temptations:

> So, if you think you are standing firm, be careful that you don't fall! No temptation has seized you except what is common to man. And God is faithful; he will not let you be tempted beyond what you can bear. But when you are tempted, he will also provide a way out so that you can stand up under it (1 Cor. 10:12–13).

2. *He pursued his desire by inquiring who Bathsheba was.* David knew that the last of the Ten Commandments said, "You shall not covet your neighbor's wife" (Exod. 20:17), and that what he was doing was wrong. Paul wrote that, in his struggle with sin, it was the commandment "Do not covet" that convicted him:

> I would not have known what sin was except through the law. For I would not have known what it was to covet if the law had not said, "Do not covet." But sin, seizing the opportunity afforded by the commandment, produced in me every kind of covetous desire. . . . I find this law at work:

When I want to do good, evil is right there with me. For in
my inner being I delight in God's law; but I see another law
at work . . . waging war against the law of my mind and
making me a prisoner of the law of sin. . . . Who will res-
cue me . . . ? Thanks be to God—through Jesus Christ our
Lord! (Rom. 7:7, 8, 21–25).

Paul is emphasizing how the very prohibition of something
stirs up and intensifies the desire for it. Paul had kept the
outward commandments diligently, but coveting is deep
in the heart, and that commandment made him see how
sinful he was.

3. He took the overt step of arranging to be with Bathsheba.
Christ explained that "anyone who looks at a woman lust-
fully has already committed adultery with her in his heart"
(Matt. 5:28). Allowing lustful desires to persist and take root
made the next step predictable, even for such a one as
David.

4. He made the decision to satisfy his desires and had sexual relations with Bathsheba. Add commandment number
seven to those David violated: "You shall not commit adultery" (Exod. 20:14). Adultery was a grave offense in Israel,
punishable by death (Lev. 20:10), if the husband chose to
press it. Paul explained to the Corinthians why sexual
immorality is so harmful:

> Flee from sexual immorality. All other sins a man com-
> mits are outside his body, but he who sins sexually sins
> against his own body. Do you not know that your body is
> a temple of the Holy Spirit, who is in you, whom you have
> received from God? You are not your own; you were bought
> at a price. Therefore honor God with your body (1 Cor.
> 6:18–20).

*5. He took Bathsheba and caused her to violate her marriage
vows* and sin along with him, thereby breaking the eighth
commandment, "You shall not steal" (Exod 20:15). He not

only stole Uriah's wife, but he also stole Bathsheba's virtue and honor. It is not clear how much blame can be laid on Bathsheba, for it would have been difficult for her to refuse the king. David misused his position of power in this self-ish venture, and the Bible clearly holds David responsible. Paul wrote to believers: "You, my brothers, were called to be free. Do not use your freedom to indulge the sinful nature; rather, serve one another in love" (Gal. 5:13).

6. *He did not admit his sin or take responsibility for it.* He tried to hide it by deceit, lying, trickery, and finally murder, now breaking the sixth and ninth commandments (Exod. 20:13, 16). In the New Testament we are advised "to put off your old self . . . which is being corrupted by its deceitful desires" (Eph. 4:22). Sin has a way of running its course unless we consciously "put on the new self, created to be like God in true righteousness and holiness" (Eph. 4:24). This is a vivid concept to keep before us as we face each new day, so that along with our usual clothing, we are conscious of "putting on" our spiritual clothing, God's provision of his righteousness. Our own won't be sufficient.

7. *He brought in Joab as an accomplice.* Joab had questionable morals anyway, and his model of a righteous man had been David. Christ said, "Let your light shine before men, that they may see your good deeds and praise your Father in heaven" (Matt. 5:16). Paul said, "Make up your mind not to put any stumbling block or obstacle in your brother's way" (Rom. 14:13).

Damaged Relationships

What a list! However, our purpose is not to get involved in condemning David but to consider how subtle sin can be as it progresses in us. It moves from the thought stage to covert actions, and then to the cover-up. We want to place the blame anywhere but on ourselves. We blame our upbringing, our personality scars from previous bad experiences, the mental or physical stress we are under, and we blame others, letting them suffer rather than facing up to the truth about ourselves. We delude ourselves by thinking, "If my sin gets out in the open, what will my friends think? I shouldn't have done it; I'm really sorry; it was a mistake, but they won't understand. They think I'm such a great Christian, and I don't want to disappoint them." We may not see it immediately, but hiding our sin ultimately has a devastating effect on our relationships with others and with God. We become less eager to pray, and we crowd out God's Word. Who wants to feel guilty all the time? So we find every excuse in the book to avoid drawing close to God.

Sin, to many, is outwardly breaking rules such as the Ten Commandments or items on a list of don'ts that our church or others have set up. When one of the scribes asked Jesus what was the greatest commandment, Jesus said, "Love the Lord your God with all your heart and with all your soul and with all your mind and with all your strength. The second is this: Love your neighbor as yourself" (Mark 12:30, 31). What Jesus was implying here is that sin begins with an attitude—an attitude in which love for self takes priority over love for God and for others. Christ was not giving new ideas that David had not known. He was putting together two Old Testament instructions God had given to Moses: Deuteronomy 6:5 and Leviticus 19:18.

When we have a question about our conduct, instead of thinking only in terms of breaking rules we must ask, "Am I acting in love?" Had David stopped and asked himself that question, and had he followed the two Old Testament commandments summarized by Christ, he would not have been drawn into breaking the rest of the commandments, which he truly loved. "If your law had not been my delight, I would have perished in my affliction. I will never forget your precepts, for by them you have renewed my life" (Ps. 119:92, 93). David did forget them, just as we do, and he refused to face what he was doing to Bathsheba, to Uriah, and to his own relationship with God.

Dangerous Detour

Can what happened to David happen to us? Why did he turn aside and take this detour from the ongoing direction of his life? Why was he so vulnerable at this time? For one whose conscience bothered him for cutting off a tiny piece of Saul's robe, something had changed. For one whose primary concern had been keeping a pure heart before God, what went wrong? Was he getting bored with his role as king? We know how wealth, prosperity, and ease can make us careless. David had always been at his best in emergencies and crises, when there were military attacks, or when his life was threatened by Saul. We, too, are often at our best in times of crisis, when our health is threatened or our loved ones are in danger, and we know only God can help.

But what about threats to our inner life with God? Are we as alert when our walk with God slips? Were David's quiet times with God less frequent now that he wasn't hiding in places like caves or a lonely desert with only God for companionship? Were his prayers mostly public, praising God for battles won, a part of formal, elaborate worship services? Were his times of meditation, which had always been a great joy, becoming "old hat" to him? We are all vulnerable at these points. Surely, David's hunger and longing for God's Word had waned. How easy it is for us to get careless when all is going well!

We see ourselves in this vivid picture of how sin takes hold, escalates, and progresses, but we want to also see ourselves in the next chapter of 2 Samuel, which records David's steps back to God after his detour into sin. It is sad that many people know much about the affair with Bathsheba, but little about David's subsequent repentance and his sense of complete cleansing and forgiveness.

David's thoughts and feelings during this period, recorded mainly in the Book of Psalms, have helped untold numbers of Christians find their way back to God when they thought their sin was too great. How could they ever again feel accepted by God? Through David's experience we can be led to repent, to confess, and to be completely assured that God has forgiven and restores us to the path of fellowship with himself. This is how the Holy Spirit works through the words of Scripture, putting them into our hearts and our actions. In this chapter and the next we have our eyes opened not only to ourselves, but also to God, to his holiness and righteousness, and to his infinite mercy and limitless love. How thankful we are that both the steps in David's failure and the steps in his return to God are spelled out for us.

Displeasure Cited

This part of the story ends with David taking Bathsheba to be his wife, and with the birth of their son. To all outward appearances, David had gotten away with his cover-up. He continued to be a popular king, and some may have thought he was noble for taking under his protection this pregnant widow whose husband had been killed in battle. But the last statement in 2 Samuel 11 is not, "And they lived happily ever after." It is rather this terse declaration: "But the thing David had done displeased the LORD."

We get the definite sense that this is not the end of the story. I have a picture of God quietly looking at his child and the tangled web he is in, waiting for the time when he will confront him. God did not throw David out on his ear. He was still the loving shepherd of Psalm 23 who would go after his sheep, even though that sheep had wandered away deliberately and gotten himself caught in a thicket. God was the same compassionate, loving, understanding God he had always been, but David's thoughts would now center on God's righteousness and holiness. David had always loved these attributes and had made them the subject of many of his hymns of praise, but now they would remind him of his sin. He knew this separated him from his God. He was truly the Lord's own; he had known the joy of being "a man after God's own heart," and he would not be able to take God's displeasure lightly.

4

God Forgives David, the Penitent Sinner

Primary Scripture Reading

2 Samuel 12
Psalm 32 and 51

Supplementary References

Isaiah 1:18
Micah 7:18, 19
Ephesians 1:7
1 John 1:9

Questions for Study and Discussion

1. Approximately how much time do you think passed between David's initial encounter with Bathsheba and the visit of Nathan the prophet in 2 Samuel 12?

   Why, do you suppose, did God wait this long to confront David?

2. Using your own words and today's language, restate the essence of the message from the Lord that Nathan relayed to David in vv. 7—10.

3. What does God imply in v. 7 and 8 is the root cause of these sins of David?

If you were David, how would you have responded to the question in v. 9?

In what ways do we sometimes despise the word of the Lord?

4. Use Psalm 51 as the basis for your devotions some morning, using David's phrases in your prayers, but applying them to your life and circumstances. On what qualities of God did David rely when he confessed his sin, and on which do you also rely?

List David's steps back to God.

What things did David ask God to do for him (see the verbs he used)?

5. Read Psalm 32, noting the negative effects of unconfessed sin, and then the positive effects of being forgiven. Why, do you suppose, had Nathan been able to reply so quickly and authoritatively in 2 Samuel 12:13, "The LORD has taken away your sin. You are not going to die"?

6. How could David say to God in Psalm 51:4, "Against you, you only, have I sinned and done what is evil in your sight," when he had done such great harm to Uriah and others?

From Psalm 51:3–6, define sin as David saw it. How did he see his own heart as he stood before God?

What hope did he have for change?

7. What are the judgments foretold by Nathan in 2 Samuel
   12:10–11?

   How do they relate to David's sins?

   Do you think such severe consequences for David's sins
   were necessary?

   Why does sin always carry sad consequences, even when
   there is complete forgiveness?

8. What do David's actions before and after the death of his
   child in 2 Samuel 12:15–23 show you about his concept of
   God?

   Did David believe in life after death? Support your answer
   from this passage.

   What do you learn about God from vv. 24 and 25?

deep bass voice from more than forty years
ago echoed in my mind as I studied 2 Samuel
12. The words I remembered were these: "I
know that my Savior has buried my sin; deep, deep in the
sea." I remember as clearly as though it were yesterday how
the rich male voice of the soloist sank lower and lower on
the scale as he approached the final word. I held my breath
to see if he would make it, and when the strong, full low
tone came forth from somewhere deep in his diaphragm,

I could visualize God taking my sin and casting it into the deepest part of the sea with authority and finality. I had the assurance that, when my sins were forgiven, they would never come back to haunt me.

Another deep voice from years ago also remains in my memory. I can still hear the voice of my father reading his favorite psalm to our family, Psalm 103, with these vivid phrases: "For as the heaven is high above the earth, so great is his mercy toward them that fear him. As far as the east is from the west, so far hath he removed our transgressions from us" (Ps. 103:11, 12 KJV). As a young child I visualized God removing my sin, and I tried to figure out how far apart east and west would be. I remember even then accepting the fact that what God did was beyond my comprehension and had something to do with infinity. These words were important to me and became a part of my life, and having studied 2 Samuel 11 and 12 for this lesson, they mean even more. They were powerful words from David, words from a man who sinned, but who experienced the mercy of God, and was profoundly grateful.

In the Bible class that I taught for many years, I had the privilege of meeting hundreds of women from many different backgrounds. My observation has been that a significant percentage came with a huge load of guilt and a very faulty understanding of the totality of God's forgiveness and cleansing. A psychiatrist friend told me that 80 percent of the problems he hears in his office can be attributed to unresolved guilt. My prayer is that this study of David's sin and restoration will give all of us a new acceptance of God's forgiveness, along with the joy and freedom from guilt that God has planned for believers.

When speaking of forgiveness, cleansing, and freedom from guilt, I am by no means belittling the seriousness of sin. We sometimes hear people joke about David's sin and use it as an excuse for their own actions: "I never did any-

thing as bad as David, and God forgave him!" But anyone who looks at David's sin should also look at David's
repentance. Yes, David's crime was terrible, but his sorrow for it was very, very deep. He failed the God who had
given him so much, but his remorse over it was of the bit-
terest kind, and the consequences were severe. Emotion-
ally, spiritually, and even physically, David seemed close
to collapse, so overcome was he by his sense of failure.
But God, in his mercy, did not abandon David. David was
overwhelmed by his sin, but he was also overwhelmed by
God's grace. He found, as we do, that God's infinite love
and compassion were far greater than his sin, and God's
forgiveness wonderfully adequate for complete cleansing.
He was profoundly grateful for God's mercy and grace, as
we are when we stray from God and experience forgiveness.

One of the things our family enjoyed most when the
children were growing up was to go camping. Our children, now grown and with families of their own, say these
are among their best memories of childhood. There is one
memory of camping, however, about which they still
laugh and complain. It is our method of awakening them
in the morning when we needed to be on the move and
they were slow in responding to our wake-up call. They
would stay snuggled in their warm sleeping bags, so we
would pull the plugs out of their air mattresses. When
they hit the hard ground, it wasn't long before they were
up and dressed, and we were on our way. George White-
field once wrote that, if you are a believer, God will put
thorns in your bed to wake you out of your complacency.
The psalmist states, "It is good for me that I have been
afflicted; that I might learn thy statutes" (Ps. 119:71 KJV).
God, in his mercy, awakened David to his unresolved guilt
and stirred him out of his complacency by sending
Nathan to him.

Confronted by Nathan

At first it seemed that David had gotten away with his sin and the subsequent cover-up. As far as his subjects were concerned, David was still a respected king busily performing his royal duties, apparently living happily in the palace with his lovely new wife and baby. It was several months before the crisis came which caused David to face up squarely to the true nature of his actions in regard to Bathsheba and Uriah. The sham might have gone on longer, but God intervened. Notice how very wise Nathan was. He did not confront David at the outset with his sin and say, "Look how you have broken Moses' commandments, you wicked king." Instead, he told David a story that could actually have happened, and the prophet could very well have been seeking David's help to right the wrong.

> The LORD sent Nathan to David. When he came to him, he said, "There were two men in a certain town, one rich and the other poor. The rich man had a very large number of sheep and cattle, but the poor man had nothing except one little ewe lamb he had bought. He raised it, and it grew up with him and his children. It shared his food, drank from his cup and even slept in his arms. It was like a daughter to him. Now a traveler came to the rich man, but the rich man refrained from taking one of his own sheep or cattle to prepare a meal for the traveler who had come to him. Instead, he took the ewe lamb that belonged to the poor man and prepared it for the one who had come to him." David burned with anger against the man and said to Nathan, "As surely as the LORD lives, the man who did this deserves to die! He must pay for that lamb four times over, because he did such a thing and had no pity" (2 Sam. 12:1–6).

Confronted by His Own Sense of Justice

David was outraged when he heard Nathan's story. To think anyone could do such a thing! He was ready to execute the man, which would be quite a harsh punishment for stealing a lamb. Then Nathan looked at David with piercing eyes, and said:

> "You are the man! This is what the LORD, the God of Israel says: 'I anointed you king over Israel, and I delivered you from the hand of Saul. I gave your master's house to you, and your master's wives into your arms. I gave you the house of Israel and Judah. And if all this had been too little, I would have given you even more. Why did you despise the word of the LORD by doing what is evil in his eyes? You struck down Uriah the Hittite with the sword . . . of the Ammonites. Now, therefore, the sword will never depart from your house, because you despised me and took the wife of Uriah the Hittite to be your own.'" . . . Then David said to Nathan, "I have sinned against the LORD" (2 Sam. 12:7–10, 13).

David was stunned when Nathan said, "You are the man!" He had condemned himself with his anger at such cruelty. As Nathan transmitted God's message and judgment, David saw his sin for what it was: sin against the God who loved him. Each phrase from Nathan must have been like a sharp knife, penetrating deeper and deeper into his heart.

Confronted by God's Goodness

Through Nathan, God first reminded David of the time when Samuel came to select one of Jesse's sons to be the future king of Israel. Although David was the youngest and least likely of all the sons to be selected, Samuel was instructed by God not to look on the outward appearance but to look on the heart. God then clearly indicated that David was his choice (1 Sam. 16:7–13). Now another prophet was sent by God to confront David and force him to look into his inner being, and to face what was there.

David's pure heart before God had always been his strength, but now he was appalled by the impurity he saw there.

David was also reminded that it was God who kept him from being killed by the hand of Saul. God had given him everything that he had; how deeply it must hurt to hear these tender words straight from God's heart, "I gave you the house of Israel and Judah, and if all this had been too little, I would have given you even more" (2 Sam. 12:8). We can imagine David abhorred his lust and his coveting of Uriah's wife at that point!

Confronted by the One True Sovereign Lord

David was stung further with this accusation: "Why did you despise the word of the LORD?" (2 Sam. 12:9). David, of all people, despise God's Word? God stated it that way, and David dared not argue. "You struck down Uriah" (v. 9). Did David kill Uriah? That's how God saw it, for he looked at David's heart, as he always had done, and "not on his outward appearance." God used the word *despised* again; this time he said, "You despised me" (v. 10).

David despised God? Isn't that a bit strong? How had he despised God? Perhaps David then thought back to the words he knew so well: "Hear, O Israel: The LORD our God, the LORD is one. Love the LORD your God with all your heart and with all your soul and with all your strength" (Deut. 6:4, 5). This is a summary of the first four of the Ten Commandments, which deal with our relationship with God and begin, "You shall have no other gods before me" (Exod. 20:3). David didn't have idols, but wasn't he putting his own desires, his own pleasure ahead of honoring God? This first commandment forms the basis for the other nine. If, indeed, Jehovah is the true God and we accept his sovereignty, then his position in our lives and hearts is to be first and preeminent. That is what makes the other nine commandments reasonable. They tell us how to live our lives in the light of who God is. To do anything less is to despise God by not giving him his rightful place in our lives.

David needed no convincing. He gave no defense. He did not try to justify his actions, or brush aside his sin by saying, "That's how it is in wartime." We see no rationalization such as, "All kings do it!" There was no anger at the prophet. The sovereign Lord was speaking to David, and David knew that every word was true and forged especially for him. He replied with one simple statement of confession: "I have sinned against the LORD" (2 Sam. 12:13). It was short, but in those few words David acknowledged that all that Nathan said was true. There were two realities for David in the statement: himself and God. He was standing before the God he loved, and he took full responsibility for what he had done.

Don't you sense relief in David's words? For many months his heart had been telling him how wrong he was, and he felt weighed down with guilt. Now it was out in the open. Those long days and long nights of hiding his sin were over.

> When I kept silent, my bones wasted away
>   through my groaning all day long.
> For day and night your hand was heavy upon me;
>   my strength was sapped as in the heat of summer.
> Then I acknowledged my sin to you
>   and did not cover up my iniquity.
> I said, "I will confess my transgressions to the LORD"—
>   and you forgave (Ps. 32:3–5).

We Are Confronted by David's Experience

Does God ever send you a Nathan—someone who speaks God's words of truth to you so they cut right to your heart? Perhaps this occurs during a sermon, or in reading a passage of Scripture. You think, "That's me! That's just what I have been doing! I didn't see it for what it was." Perhaps with horror you realize, "I've been jealous of that person. I can't believe it. I thought I was beyond that. I've never been prone to jealousy, but that's exactly what it is. That's why I have been feeling this way toward that person." You suddenly know your problem is pride, selfishness, dishonesty, or desire for malicious gossip.

When we come into the presence of a holy God, we clearly see our sin for what it is, how it has hurt others, but most of all that it is sin against God. John Calvin said that as long as our gaze is fixed on the ground, we are safe. But when we look at God, we are awestruck by the thought, "How could I do this to the God who has given me so much?" His blessings flood our minds, and we are confronted with his infinite love and kindnesses to us, just as David was. When God sends you a Nathan, do you listen and say with David, "I have sinned against God"? Continuing confession and realization of our need of cleansing in the presence of our holy Lord is the foundation of a good relationship with God.

If we had only the historical record in 2 Samuel, we would not know David's thoughts and emotions at this time, or his words when he repented and cried out to God for cleansing. Fortunately, we are not left with only this narrative; we have David's words in Psalm 32 and 51 as he pours out his heart. Throughout this study of David, we have related appropriate psalms to events in David's life and tried to gain insight into his heart and mind through them. At this time of heartbreak and deep repentance, David penned some of his most powerful and meaningful psalms. As he faced the magnitude of his sin and struggled with his sense of failure, he was disgusted and repelled by what he saw in himself. The prayers in his psalms express his longing to be forgiven and to be restored to fellowship.

Perhaps no other psalm has been of greater help to us than Psalm 51. When we stray from God, we wonder how

God's mercy and grace could possibly be stretched enough to forgive sins such as ours. We, with David, long to have our fellowship with God restored. In Psalm 51 we have laid out for us David's steps back to God: how he approached God, how he saw himself, and how he saw God. We can identify with David in his conviction of sin, his confession, and his prayer for pardon. While we sincerely work through these steps, we, too, can experience cleansing and complete restoration, no matter what the magnitude of our sins:

> A psalm of David.
> When the prophet Nathan
> came to him after he had committed
> adultery with Bathsheba.
>
> Have mercy on me, O God,
>   according to your unfailing love;
> according to your great compassion
>   blot out my transgressions.
> Wash away all my iniquity
>   and cleanse me from my sin.
> For I know my transgressions,
>   and my sin is always before me
>   (Ps. 51:1–3).

1. David asked for forgiveness on the basis of God's character. David asked first of all for God's mercy—not because he deserved it, not because he was sorry enough, and not because of anything good in himself. He dared approach God for one reason only: his faith in God's mercy. He was not asking for justice; he was asking to be treated in accord with God's character—God's unfailing love and the deep well of his compassion, mercy, and grace. He could approach God because of his assurance of what God was, not what he himself was. It was not a matter of whether David could work up enough guilt and remorse to satisfy

an angry God, or whether he could flagellate himself suf-
ficiently. There was no way David could work his way back
into God's good graces, and he knew it. Forgiveness for
David rested totally on the quality and depth of God's
mercy; this was his hope, and this is our hope. This is the
only basis on which David or any of us dares to come to
God, no matter how big or little our crimes.

   2. *David accepted total responsibility for his sin.* David's
confession was thorough. Look at the guilt he felt in Psalm
51. He knew that his record with God had been ruined. He
wanted God to "blot out" his sin from whatever records
were kept. Whenever he tried to come to God, his sin
loomed up so that was all he could see ("My sin is always
before me"). He felt the immensity of his sins as he said,
"Wash away *all* my iniquity." Notice the use of the personal pronouns *I, me,* and *my.* David was not praying about
the sin of others; rather, it was as though he stood alone
before God and pleaded guilty to all charges: "I know my
transgressions."

   Modern psychology warns us that guilt is very bad for
our health and emotional well-being and that we should
get rid of it because of all of the destructive things it does
to us. The Bible would agree with that, and we have only
to see what guilt did to David to know its devastating and
debilitating effects. But guilt can be a friend as well as a foe
if we see it as a warning that something is wrong. It can
signal to us that we need to go to God to let him show us
the true nature of our problem and to let him provide the
way to remove our guilt. He alone can do this.

   Psychologists tell us we need to distinguish between true
guilt and false guilt. False guilt is something laid on us by
other people. For example, we can be made to feel guilty
if we don't measure up to someone else's standards. Or
maybe you have someone near you who tries to manipu-
late you by making you feel guilty. That is not what we
mean by true guilt before God. When we sin, we don't

merely feel guilty, we *are* guilty, and we know it! How did God bring David to see this point? He did it through his very own words to David, which like an X-ray machine revealed the malignant spots in David. God's Word will do the same for us today.

3. David acknowledged that his sin was against God:

Against you, you only have I sinned
 and done what is evil in your sight
 so that you are proved right when you speak
 and justified when you judge.
Surely I have been a sinner from birth,
 sinful from the time my mother conceived me.
Surely you desire truth in the inner parts;
 you teach me wisdom in the inmost place (Ps. 51:4–6).

David saw his sin as rebellion against God. He knew he had wronged Uriah and a lot of other people, and he knew it was sin to injure others, because it goes against God's commandments. David was so overcome by the way he had sinned against God that his wrongs against others were included and blended in with his confession to God. Notice that he was not focusing on the punishment or the consequences of his sin, which would turn out to be enormous, but he was focusing on God. He mourned his sin because it displeased God. Can't you imagine David on his knees, tears flowing, as he worshiped God for his righteousness, his fairness, and his holiness (v. 4)? He recognized that God desired truth in the innermost part of his being (v. 6), and was teaching him about his own nature as well as about God's nature.

4. David saw sin as a permeating condition, not just deeds. As David honestly confronted his sin, he saw how deeply rooted it was. He discovered that it was inbred and touched every aspect of his nature and personality; he saw that his actions flowed from a heart that was inclined against God.

Until we see sin as it truly is, as a falling short of God's glory in every aspect of our lives, we will fail to grasp its power and thereby fail to appreciate how great is God's mercy and how marvelous is Christ's work of redemption for us.

5. *David asked God for complete cleansing:*

> Cleanse me with hyssop, and I will be clean;
>   wash me, and I will be whiter than snow.
> Let me hear joy and gladness;
>   let the bones you have crushed rejoice.
> Hide your face from my sin
>   and blot out all my iniquity.
> Create in me a pure heart, O God,
>   and renew a steadfast spirit within me (Ps. 51:7–10).

David felt contaminated and filthy, and longed for God to cleanse him. Four times he asked for cleansing, expressing not only the idea of washing dirty garments, which was required for the priests before coming into God's presence (v. 2), but also the ceremonial cleansing performed in the temple by the priests, as suggested by the use of hyssop (see Exod. 12:22 and Lev. 14:4, 6). Hyssop was used when a former leper, who had been cured or incorrectly diagnosed, was declared clean and ready to be accepted back into the assembly of God's people, with all rights and privileges restored. David wanted the symbolic cleansing of his outer garments so he could come into God's presence. He also longed for the purification of his innermost spirit and the removal of the pollution that had permeated his being.

When David prayed for such thorough cleansing, he may have been exhibiting greater faith than in any other part of this psalm, considering the nature of sin and his understanding of it. Isn't this also true for us? It takes faith to believe that Christ, through his atoning death, can apply his blood to our sin so that it can be taken away and each of us can pray, "Wash me, and I will be whiter than snow." God promises to do just that in these words to us through Isaiah: "'Come now, and let us reason together,' says the LORD. 'Though your sins are like scarlet, they shall be as white as snow; though they are red as crimson, they shall be like wool'" (Isa. 1:18). That is God's mercy in action, secured for us by Christ's death on the cross, so that we can claim these New Testament promises:

> If we confess our sins, he is faithful and just and will for-give us our sins and purify us from all unrighteousness (1 John 1:9). In him we have redemption through his blood, the forgiveness of sin, in accordance with the riches of God's grace that he lavished upon us with all wisdom and under-standing (Eph. 1:7, 8).

In America we often forget what a luxury it is to be able to maintain high standards of cleanliness. We are told that one of the greatest hardships for prisoners of war and inmates of concentration camps is to be deprived of ways to keep clean. A dear friend, a fastidious Englishwoman who was interned as a prisoner by the Japanese in World War II, said that only someone who has been through it can appreciate how it lowers one's self-esteem and sense of dignity as a human being to be without ways of keeping clean.

Up to the time of David's sin in 2 Samuel 11, he had given every evidence of being a spiritually fastidious per-son, considering himself acceptable to God and enjoying coming into God's presence because his heart was clean. Listen to some of his own words:

> I have kept myself
>   from the ways of the violent.
> My steps have held to your paths;
>   my feet have not slipped (Ps. 17:4, 5).

I have trusted in the LORD
without wavering.
Test me, O LORD, and try me,
examine my heart and my mind;
for your love is ever before me,
and I walk continually in your truth (Ps. 26:1–3).

The LORD has dealt with
me according to my righteousness;
According to the cleanness of my hands,
he has rewarded me (Ps. 18:20).

Previously, David had seen clearly that he couldn't get away with living like those around him. He knew that he had been chosen by God and had been given the Holy Spirit in a special way. He was aware that he lived his life in the presence of God and under the eyes of God. Yet, it had never seemed to be a burden, so confident was he of God's love and approval. He was comfortable with his responsibility to live a clean life and to walk according to the truth as God had given it. These are the things he here remembered, and which he knew he had lost. What a contrast between David's attitude in Psalm 18 and 51 and the other penitential psalms.[1] What broke David's heart was that he had deliberately damaged the relationship with God he had always treasured. He prayed that God would still give him his presence and not remove his Holy Spirit from him (Ps. 51:11).

6. *David asked for joy.* David asked God, "Let me hear joy and gladness; let the bones you have crushed rejoice" (Ps. 51:8). He prayed, "Restore to me the joy of your salvation" (v. 12). Nehemiah used these words to encourage the hard workers who were repairing the walls of Jerusalem, "The joy of the LORD is your strength" (Neh. 8:10). The words *joy* and

1. There are seven psalms that early Christian liturgy classified as penitential psalms. The other five are Psalm 6, 32, 102, 130, and 143.

rejoice are also key words in Paul's writings. Paul saw joy as an important outworking of God in the Christian. He told the Philippians: "Rejoice in the Lord always. I will say it again: Rejoice!" (Phil. 4:4). To the Galatians he wrote, "What has happened to all your joy?" (Gal. 4:15). He listed joy as one of the fruits of the Spirit (Gal. 5:22). David is indeed scriptural when he prays for joy, and so are we. What greater joy is there than to experience the mercy of God as he cleanses our hearts? When you feel no strength of your own, when things seem heavy or impossible, or as you begin a new day, try asking for joy, and see if it isn't one of the most strengthening things God gives you.

7. *David asked God to give him a new heart.* God had originally chosen David because of his heart (1 Sam. 16:7). Now David wanted God to use his creative power to give him new attitudes, new purposes, new emotions—in short, "a pure heart" (Ps. 51:10). He asked for a steadfast spirit (v. 10), and a willing spirit (v. 12). He prayed, "The sacrifices of God are a broken spirit; a broken and contrite heart, O God, you will not despise" (v. 17). David felt he was despicable in God's sight, and the only hope he saw was for God to create a new heart in him, one that God could accept and love. Isn't that the paradox of the Christian life? We please God most if we let him provide everything and allow him to work out his salvation in us, rather than trying to earn his favor by our own efforts.

8. *David prayed for others:*

> Then I will teach transgressors your ways,
>   and sinners will turn back to you. . . .
> My tongue will sing of your righteousness.
> O LORD, open my lips,
>   and my mouth will declare your praise. . . .
> In your good pleasure make Zion prosper;
>   build up the walls of Jerusalem.
> Then there will be righteous sacrifices (Ps. 51:5, 18–19).

We see hope returning to David. He wanted God to use him again, and he wanted to praise God with all of his heart—the new, pure heart God gave him. David's steps back into fellowship with God were complete when his joy spilled over and he wanted to share his joy and praise with others. David had genuine assurance he was forgiven. He felt his sins were hurled into the depths of the sea, removed as far as the east is from the west. His joy returned, and he felt surrounded by God's love and mercy.

> Who is a God like you,
>> who pardons sin and forgives the transgression
>> of the remnant of his inheritance?
> You do not stay angry forever
>> but delight to show mercy.
> You will again have compassion on us . . .
>> and hurl our iniquities into the depths of the sea (Mic. 7:18–19).

Do we know that God forgave David? Listen to these words of David:

> Blessed is he
>> whose transgressions are forgiven,
>> whose sin is covered.
> Blessed is the man
>> whose sin the LORD does not count against him
>> and in whose spirit there is no deceit. . . .
> I said, "I will confess
>> my transgressions to the LORD"—
>> and you forgave the guilt of my sin. . . .
> Many are the woes of the wicked,
>> but the LORD's unfailing love
>> surrounds the man who trusts in him (Ps. 32:1, 2, 5, 6, 10).

5

God Comforts David, the Troubled Father

Primary Scripture Reading	Supplementary References
2 Samuel 3:1–5; 12:24, 25; 13:1–20:26	2 Samuel 22 1 Kings 1:1–3:15

Questions for Study and Discussion

1. Chapters 13 through 20 of 2 Samuel describe some very hard years for David, years of dealing with deception, intrigue, and sorrow. Read through these chapters quickly, as you would any absorbing story. Notice that, in spite of trying circumstances, David stood out among his contemporaries as a man of faith with a close walk with God.

2. Carefully review the listing of David's wives and their children given in 1 Samuel 18:20–29, and 2 Samuel 6:23; 3:2–5; 11:26; 12:24. Which names do you recognize?

   How were the various judgments of God against David, given by Nathan in 2 Samuel 12:10–12, fulfilled literally later in David's life?

   For your answer see 2 Samuel 13:1–21; 13:28–33; 16:20–22; 18:9–16; and 1 Kings 2:22–25.

81

3. In each of the following passages, find what Absalom actually asked or said and what appears to be his unstated purpose: 2 Samuel 13:20–22; 13:23–29; 15:7–12. What, do you think, was Absalom's opinion of his father?

Based on David's past, why was he so lenient with both Amnon and Absalom?

4. What do you find striking about David's behavior in the events recorded in 2 Samuel 15:1–12?

How did David deal with defeat and humiliation in each of the following passages: 2 Samuel 15:13–23; 15:24–26; 16:5–13? What clever initiatives did David take in 2 Samuel 15:32–37 to get information from Absalom's headquarters?

What does 2 Samuel 15:25–26 show you about David's relationship with God?

5. How did David's soldiers, as well as others, respond to him in 2 Samuel 15:19–22; 17:15–22; 17:27–29; 18:1–4?

What do we have to do to gain such a reputation?

Why did Joab kill Absalom in spite of David's request to spare his son's life?

What was Joab's opinion of David?

6. Of the events in 2 Samuel 19, what impresses you about David's character? What possible weaknesses do you see?

Read the conflicting stories told to David in 2 Samuel 16:1–4; 19:17–18; 19:24–30. Whom do you believe, Ziba or Mephibosheth?

Why, do you suppose, David in the end divided the land equally?

7. Read 1 Chronicles 22:7–13. What things did David want most for his son Solomon?

*S*ome children are rebellious, as we know all too well. If you haven't raised any yourself, you've seen enough little monsters in grocery stores or restaurants, or bigger monsters cruising around with stereos blaring full blast, to be sympathetic with their frustrated parents.

David also had problems with his children, especially with the deceitful, rebellious Absalom. The record of David's experiences with his children gives us an opportunity to observe his role as father, and to consider ways to avoid his problems and to strengthen our own family relationships. To understand the relationships and difficulties between David and his children and among the children themselves, it helps to try to picture the way they lived. Contrary to God's model in Genesis 2:24, which says, "For this reason a man will leave his father and mother and be united to his wife and they shall become one flesh," David had many wives and concubines. This was a common practice in that day and was considered a sign of wealth and power. Moreover, there was an apparent precedent for this, going back to the patriarchs. Abraham had one principal wife, Sarah, but took Sarah's maid Hagar to be his concubine and had a child by her. Jacob married both Leah and Rachel and in addition fathered children by several concubines. But in each of these situations jealousy and trouble erupted between the wives and between the children, so the danger of departing from God's model was there for all to see.

Six of David's wives and each of their firstborn sons, all of which were born in Hebron, are listed in 2 Samuel 3:2–5. The list omits Michal, Saul's daughter whom he married earlier and who bore him no children, and omits Bathsheba, mother of Solomon, whom he married later, as well as some others who are not named here (2 Sam. 5:13–16). In the palace compound where they all lived, each wife undoubtedly lived with her own children and provided the primary care for them, especially in their early years. As the children grew, they were probably taught in groups by priests and teachers. David may have watched his children play and perhaps participated. He may also have played his harp or lute for them, singing the songs and poems he wrote as a shepherd or when hiding in lonely places from Saul. Nevertheless, considering this situation it is not hard to imagine that David's relationship as a father to his children was much more distant and formal than is common today, and that jealousy and rivalries could easily have arisen among the siblings. David's military campaigns and the problems of governing his people would also have kept him away from his children, making each of their mother's influence all the more important. The children, in turn, must have felt mutual kinship as David's offspring, while at the same time recognizing the distinction between their full and half brothers and sisters.

The middle years of David's life, during which he had problems with his sons, were indeed hectic. We cannot say for sure what was going on in his mind at this time, but looking at the events of these years together with what David wrote in the psalms provides useful insights into what he was feeling and how God comforted him and helped him cope with all the turmoil.

David's firstborn son was Amnon; his second was Kileab, son of Abigail, widow of Nabal; his third was Absalom, whose mother was Maacah, a pagan princess and the daughter of the foreign king Talmai of Geshur, a kingdom to the north of Israel; and his fourth was Adonijah. These four, along with Solomon, are the sons involved in the events recorded in 2 Samuel, with the spotlight focused on Absalom, whose violent life was filled with hatred, deceit, murder, and rebellion—soap-opera material!

Trouble in the Family

It all began with David's beautiful daughter, Tamar, who was Absalom's full sister. Amnon, her half brother, who as the oldest son would have been considered the crown prince, fell madly in love with Tamar. He was so smitten by Tamar that he couldn't eat or sleep. After concocting a ruse so that he would be alone with the lovely Tamar in his bedroom, Amnon forcibly raped her over her protest that "such a thing should not be done in Israel," and then threw her out in disgrace and would have nothing more to do with her. Absalom was justifiably enraged over the rape of his sister and began to plot his revenge.

David was furious when he heard of this affair, but what did he do about it? The Bible says nothing about any punishment meted out to Amnon. One wonders if David felt compromised and weakened because of his own adulterous affair with Bathsheba and was incapable of expressing appropriate "tough love" and discipline because of this. Perhaps communication with his children was one of David's problems, as it is with many fathers today. If David had discussed the heinousness of the crime with his children, especially with Tamar's brother Absalom, and then punished appropriately, things might have turned out differently. Absalom's anger might have been assuaged. Notice what a devious schemer Absalom was! He always seemed to have a hidden agenda! In his conversations with Tamar and later with David, he never let on what was his real motive. He told Tamar to cool it, to "be quiet now, my sister; he is your brother. Don't take this thing to heart" (2 Sam. 13:20). But in his own heart his hatred for Amnon and desire for revenge continued to fester. It took two years for Absalom to find the right moment to get even. The occasion he chose was a big party to wind up the annual sheep-shearing season at his ranch in Ephraim. He first invited his father, David, and the royal officers, probably knowing they wouldn't come because Ephraim was quite far from Jerusalem. What did he do next? After being turned down, he begged David, "Please let my brother Amnon come with us." David hesitated, aware of bad feelings between them, but in the end agreed to let Amnon go and, in fact, sent all his sons along with Absalom. Absalom's plan was ready; he arranged with his servants to kill Amnon at the height of the party when everyone would be having a good time, then assured them that he would protect them from punishment. So Absalom gained his long-awaited revenge through this treachery, and he also eliminated an older brother who was ahead of him in the line of succession to the throne.

David wept bitterly when he heard the news. Perhaps David saw this as a partial fulfillment of Nathan's prophecy, "Now, therefore, the sword will never depart from your house. . . . Out of your own household I am going to bring calamity upon you. Before your very eyes I will take your wives and give them to one who is close to you, and he will lie with your wives in broad daylight" (2 Sam. 12:10–11). Was it his fault this was happening? Was he as much to blame as Absalom? Absalom, however, wasn't sure what his father would do to him, and so fled to Geshur, his mother's home country. Absalom stayed there in exile for three years, while "David mourned for his son every day" and longed for his return.

Another schemer now entered the picture. Joab, David's general, saw that David's sorrow and longing for Absalom were crippling him as king, so he devised a scheme to convince David to let Absalom return home. He hoped this would lift David out of his depression. He hired a woman to tell David a sad story in which she said she was a widow in danger of losing her only remaining son who had gotten into a fight with his brother and killed him. Her neighbors now demanded that the offending son be put to death for his crime, which would leave the poor woman without any family or support. As Joab suspected, David's sensitive heart was touched by the story. The woman then skillfully turned the story around to apply it to David's treatment of Absalom. David got the point, and agreed that Absalom could return home. But then he did a strange thing; he said that Absalom must not see his face. For two years Absalom was in Jerusalem, but did not meet his father. Joab saw this was a bad situation, and finally talked David into seeing his son. The reunion seemed genuine; Absalom acted properly humble and contrite, and David kissed him.

Treachery Continues

Did they live happily ever after? Oh, no, not Absalom! He still wanted to be king and grew even bolder. Instead of appreciating and valuing his father's great love and forgiving spirit, he seemed to despise him all the more. Those were not traits he admired. He began an intensive, clever campaign to ingratiate himself to the people and eventually "stole the hearts of the men of Israel" away from David. Absalom was really good looking: "In all Israel there was not a man so highly praised for his handsome appearance as Absalom. From the top of his head to the sole of his foot there was no blemish in him" (2 Sam. 14:25). And he put on quite a show! He paraded around in a fancy chariot and had fifty lackeys run ahead of him to attract attention. The handsome prince with his beautiful flowing hair cunningly began to curry the favor of the people:

> He would get up early and stand by the side of the road leading to the city gate. Whenever anyone came with a complaint to be placed before the king for a decision, Absalom would call out to him, "What town are you from?" He would answer, "Your servant is from one of the tribes of Israel." Then Absalom would say to him, "Look, your claims are valid and proper, but there is no representative of the king to hear you." And Absalom would add, "If only I were appointed judge in the land! Then everyone who has a complaint or case could come to me and I would see that he gets justice" (2 Sam. 15:2–4).

What a slick politician! But where was David at this time? Was there really a breakdown in his leadership? Why wasn't he dispensing justice and meeting these evident needs, so that Absalom would not have been able to move into this vacuum?

After four years of campaigning, Absalom felt all was ready for him to make his big move. Many people gullibly swallowed his line, and even part of the army supported him. So he went to David with another subtle lie. He piously proposed, "Let me go to Hebron and fulfill a vow I made to the LORD. While your servant was living at Geshur in Aram, I made this vow: 'If the LORD takes me back to Jerusalem, I will worship the LORD in Hebron'" (2 Sam. 15:7–8). David welcomed this glimmer of religious interest and said, "Go in peace." But what was Absalom's true intention? To rebel and take over the kingdom! Why Hebron? He apparently thought it would be symbolic, if not ironic, to announce from Hebron that he was the new king, for this was the very city from which David first reigned as king before Jerusalem was conquered and made the capital (2 Sam. 5). When David heard the news of the rebellion, he realized he was totally unprepared. He didn't know how much military support he still had, nor how much Absalom possessed and so decided to give up Jerusalem, his beloved capital city, without a fight, perhaps to spare the city from destruction and bloodshed. He fled with his household and loyal followers to the northeast and then across the Jordan.

What a sad procession left Jerusalem that day, most of them on foot. "The whole countryside wept aloud as all the people passed by . . . and . . . moved on toward the desert" (2 Sam. 15:23). David, too, wept as he trudged along, but he was calm and resolute, his trust in his God never wavering. The Levites had brought along the ark of the covenant, but David told faithful Zadok the priest to take it back to Jerusalem, saying, "If I find favor in the LORD's eyes, he will bring me back and let me see it and his dwelling place again. But if he says, 'I am not pleased with you' then I am ready; let him do to me whatever seems good to him" (2 Sam. 15:25–26).

How discouraged and forsaken he must have felt! For one who had such pure, godly motives, one who was sensitive and tender, the hurt must have been nearly intolerable. How could he stand it? His psalms clearly show how keenly he felt the hurt and pain, and also how he was able to pour out his heart to God. In Psalm 62, which may have expressed his thoughts at this time, David laid out his distress before God:

> How long will you assault a man?
> Would all of you throw him down—
> this leaning wall, this tottering fence?
> They fully intend to topple him

from his lofty place;
they take delight in lies.
With their mouths they bless,
but in their hearts they curse (Ps. 62:3–4).

David had borne about as much as any man could. He was close to losing his family, his throne, and even his life; but he knew he was not alone. He knew he could talk to his Lord and lay out before him all of his thoughts and feelings. Yes, some of these calamities may have been his own fault, but David seemed to grasp even then the truth, "Whom the Lord loveth he chasteneth" (Heb. 12:6 KJV). To David, God's love was real; the more he prayed and called out to God, the more he felt God's love surrounding him. Notice how his trust in the goodness of the character of God stirred David's heart as he continues in this psalm:

Find rest, O my soul, in God alone;
my hope comes from him.
He alone is my rock and my salvation;
he is my fortress, I will not be shaken.
My salvation and my honor depend on God;
he is my mighty rock, my refuge.
Trust in him at all times, O people;
pour out your hearts to him,
for God is our refuge (Ps. 62:5, 8).

In this psalm and others, we find a change of perspective as David with total honesty poured out his true feelings to God. David's problems grew smaller and less important, while the majesty and power of God grew in David's mind until he felt overwhelmed with praise. Have you discovered this principle and do you practice it when you feel your problems are more than you can bear? Would you try it today? As you concentrate on who God is and praise him for his character, you will find your spirits lifted as you face your problems with his perspective and a renewed sense of hope. Using the words of David in the psalms and knowing the difficulties he faced help us develop this habit.

Meanwhile, back in Jerusalem Absalom had taken over the royal palace and considered what he should do next to consolidate his power. Now the plot thickens! Although he didn't know it, he was headed for disaster, for David had sent his own trusted counselor, Hushai, back to Jerusalem to serve as a double agent, pretending to have switched allegiance to Absalom. His real mission, however, was to counteract the advice of Ahithophel, Absalom's brilliant and cunning advisor, and to act as a spy for David. Ahithophel advised Absalom first to possess publicly David's concubines who had been left behind to watch over the palace. This symbolic act, which seems strange to us, signified that a new king had taken over. Unbeknownst to Absalom and the people, it also fulfilled part of Nathan's earlier prophecy. Ahithophel then advised Absalom to take his present army of twelve thousand men and pursue David immediately, while David was still weary and disorganized, and to "strike down only the king." Absalom was inclined to do this, but decided to ask Hushai what he thought of the plan. "The advice Ahithophel has given is not good this time," said Hushai, becoming eloquent. "Let all Israel, from Dan to Beersheba—as numerous as the sand on the seashore—be gathered to you, with you yourself leading them into battle. Then we will attack him wherever he may be found, and we will fall on him as dew settles on the ground. Neither he nor any of his men will be left alive" (2 Sam. 17:11–12). Hushai's idea sounded great to the vain Absalom, and he adopted it.

Treason Rewarded

David was now getting help from another source. Many of his experienced fighting men still loved and respected their king who had led them to so many victories. Upon hearing the news of Absalom's rebellion they filtered through the countryside to join his army. By the time Absalom had gathered his forces and was ready to strike, David was also prepared, reluctantly, to fight against his son. As he sent his troops into battle, David gave specific instructions to his commanders, "Be gentle with the young man Absalom for my sake." The great battle took place in a forest in Ephraim, a site probably chosen by David so that the chariots and horses of Absalom's army would be useless. It was a bloody, decisive battle with twenty thousand casualties, and David's men defeated and scattered Absalom's army.

Absalom tried to escape David's men in the dense forest, but his hair, or his head, got caught in the branches, pulling him off his mount and leaving him dangling in midair. He was found by one of David's soldiers who remembered David's words and so did not harm him. He made the mistake of telling his commander Joab about it. Joab immediately went to where Absalom was hanging and killed him, then took down the body and buried it in a pit, covering it with a large pile of rocks.

Why did Joab deliberately disobey the command of the king for whom he had risked his life many times in battle and to whom he was intensely loyal? Perhaps it was because he felt betrayed by Absalom, since he was the one who had convinced David to let Absalom return from exile and later arranged their reconciliation. Perhaps it was because he thought David was too soft and forgiving with Absalom, and that for David's own good, he (Joab) should take matters into his own hands and give this ungrateful traitor his just reward, lest he escape scot-free yet again. Regardless of Joab's motives, David was overcome with grief when he heard the news of Absalom's death; he wept bitterly and moaned, "O my son Absalom! My son, my son Absalom! If only I had died instead of you—O Absalom, my son, my son!" (2 Sam. 18:33). Many a father would have rejected a son like Absalom long before, but David's love and forgiveness seemed to know no bounds. He had experienced God's forgiveness, and in this situation he was reflecting God's fatherlike love. Does the forgiveness you have received enable you to show grace to those who wrong you?

David's great grief over the death of Absalom was very evident to his soldiers. Was he more concerned about the death of his rebellious son than he was about the great victory gained on the battlefield at the risk of their lives? This seeming ingratitude angered Joab, who went to David and upbraided him with these harsh words:

> Today you have humiliated all your men, who have just saved your life and the lives of your sons and daughters and the lives of your wives and concubines. You love those who hate you and hate those who love you. You have made it clear today that the commanders and their men mean nothing to you. I see that you would be pleased if Absalom were alive today and all of us were dead. Now go out and encourage your men. I swear by the LORD that if you don't go out, not a man will be left with you by nightfall. This will be worse for you than all the calamities that have come upon you from your youth till now (2 Sam. 19:5–7).

David accepted this rebuke from his general, met with his men to thank them, and then returned to Jerusalem.

Training Neglected?

Looking back over these chapters in 2 Samuel on Absalom's life, one wonders what went wrong. Why did Absalom not admire and seek to emulate his father? Why was David so blind and so lenient with his rebellious son? Couldn't he see that Absalom was a schemer from day one? Shouldn't David have realized this, beginning with Absalom's deception and murder of Amnon? Surely, someone must have told David about Absalom's brazen attempts over a four-year period to steal the hearts of the people after he returned from exile; yet David appeared to suspect nothing, or at least did nothing to protect his own interests. Could it have been because David himself was so honest, trusting, and straightforward that he never suspected opposite traits in his handsome son? Was it because David felt so profoundly his own forgiveness by God after his sin with Bathsheba, that he could not bring himself to punish Absalom, even when such punishment and discipline were really needed? Also, was it not a pattern of David's life, so evident when he was being pursued by Saul, not to take matters into his own hands but rather to trust the Lord to work things out for him in the Lord's own way and time? We can only speculate on these questions, but one thing is certain, the record has much to teach us.

David and Absalom seemed not to be able to communicate or to understand each other at a deep level. A strong father-son relationship never developed between them under the living conditions in the king's palace. Perhaps younger brother Solomon was referring to this hurtful situation later when he wrote in Proverbs 22:6, "Train a child in the way he should go, and when he is old he will not turn from it," and again in Proverbs 13:1, "A wise son heeds his father's instruction, but a mocker does not listen to rebuke." By the time Absalom was an adult, he was too self-centered, egotistical, and ambitious to listen to his father or to consider anyone's welfare but his own. His only goal seemed to be to destroy anyone who stood between him and the throne.

David's problems with his children did not end with the death of Absalom. His fourth son, Adonijah, next oldest after Absalom, was yet to rebel. He tried to take over the throne when David was old and weak. David nipped this one in the bud by moving quickly to have the young Solomon anointed king publicly, with trumpets blaring and the crowd shouting, "Long live King Solomon." Adonijah's followers, who included Joab, heard the clamor and deserted him. He was later put to death by Solomon, making him the third of David's sons to die by the sword. How terribly sad for David; but God gave him great joy in his son Solomon.

The Torch Passes

Solomon was a son David could be proud of—a fine successor to the throne! He exhibited excellent values, great wisdom, and strong faith in God. Why did he turn out so well? It is beautiful to see how David drew even closer to the Lord in his later years and made preparations for Solomon to build the temple in Jerusalem. He shared his excitement and insights with young Solomon, and did everything he could to teach him what it meant to be a leader under God and to prepare and equip him to be king.

David's faith in God was strong all through his life, especially at the beginning and at the end. But aren't we grateful that those difficult middle years are recorded? It helps us with our problems and enables us to understand that even the best of us can fall into sin, but that God forgives completely when we repent, and restores us to our former relationship with him, showing us that his character is unchanging.

Near the end of his life, just before he died, David gave a beautiful, challenging message from his heart to Solomon:

> My son, I had it in my heart to build a house for the Name of the Lord my God. But this word of the Lord came to me: "You have shed much blood and have fought many wars. You are not to build a house for my Name, because you have shed much blood on the earth in my sight. But you will have a son who will be a man of peace and rest, and I will give him rest from all his enemies on every side.

His name will be Solomon, and I will grant Israel peace and quiet during his reign. He is the one who will build a house for my Name. He will be my son, and I will be his father. And I will establish the throne of his kingdom over Israel forever." Now, my son, the LORD be with you, and may you have success and build the house of the LORD your God, as he said you would. May the LORD give you discretion and understanding when he puts you in command over Israel, so that you may keep the law of the LORD your God. Then you will have success if you are careful to observe the decrees and laws that the LORD gave Moses for Israel. Be strong and courageous. Do not be afraid or discouraged (1 Chron. 22:7–13).

Later, after Solomon completed the temple and had the ark of the covenant placed in it, Jehovah came and filled the temple with his presence in a spectacular way, confirming that he was pleased with this wise young king, and that this son of David had indeed been well-prepared and instructed by his father, even under difficult circumstances.

Today's Challenge

Today we don't have marriages with multiple wives and concubines, but we do have divorces, and in some cases multiple divorces involving the same parent. These situations tend to exacerbate the problems of jealousy, rivalry, and lack of communication that are present to some extent in all families. Bringing up children today is tough, even under the best circumstances. Whatever our situation, with or without divorce, it is essential in all families for parents and children to maintain communication. Are you as a parent making it a point to communicate with your children? Are you trying to stay close enough to your children to share thoughts and ideas with them, to let them know your concerns, problems, and joys, as well as encouraging them to share theirs? Are you then praying with them and studying the Bible together to gain wisdom to know what to do about these problems? Do you know your children well enough to sense what is going on in their lives and in their relationships, to encourage them in what is good and worthwhile, and to discourage what is dangerous and bad by confronting them about such things, perhaps with tears and prayer, but always with honesty, love, and firmness? Are you exhibiting David's strong qualities of faith, hope, love, and prayer before your children, while at the same time avoiding his failure to be close to them and to confront and discipline them when that is needed?

Your own relationship with the Lord is basic to successful relationships with your spouse and with your children. Just as David discovered, your faith and trust in God will help you keep your perspective and joy, even when you feel overwhelmed by problems. When you're feeling low and discouraged, think of David's difficulties and then read 2 Samuel 22 again. You, too, will receive God's comfort!

> The LORD is my rock, my fortress and my deliverer;
>   my God is my rock, in whom I take refuge;
>   my shield and the horn of my salvation.
> He is my stronghold, my refuge and my savior—
>   from violent men you save me.
> I call to the LORD, who is worthy of praise,
>   and I am saved from my enemies (2 Sam. 22:2–4).

6

God Completes David, the Continuing King

Primary Scripture Readings

1 Chronicles 28, 29;
2 Samuel 7

Supplementary References

Psalm 100
Isaiah 55:3
Luke 1:32
Acts 13:22, 23, 34–36
Revelation 21:1–3

Questions for Study and Discussion

1. Read 1 Chronicles 28 and 29, and try to visualize the dramatic scene. Describe the assembled group.

   Why were they present?

   What do you see as David's purposes for the gathering?

2. Why was David so eager to build a temple (see 2 Sam. 7)?

   Why did God's refusal of his request to build the temple bring such joy to David?

99

What effect did this encounter with God have on David throughout the rest of his reign?

Do you find any evidence it affected David's attitude toward the future?

3. Why, do you suppose, did David relate so many details about his former encounter with God, recorded in 1 Chronicles 28?

How would you describe David's emotions in 1 Chronicles 28 and 29 as he contemplated turning the throne over to Solomon?

4. List the ways David showed a father's concern for a son who was taking over the reins of the kingdom from him. List the ways David smoothed the way for an orderly transition of power to Solomon.

How did David try to promote in the people a positive attitude toward Solomon? Was he successful (1 Chron. 29:22–25)?

5. What would the anticipation of building the temple do for the people as they began to live under a new monarch?

In what way did they follow David's example in providing for the temple (1 Chron. 29:6–9)?

Which emotions were brought forth by the generosity of both David and the other leaders?

6. Try to capture David's deepest desires for his son and for the people. Fill in a chart, using David's words of encouragement and exhortation for public and private life.

Charge to the People (1 Chron. 28:8)	*Charge to Solomon* (1 Chron. 28:9, 10, 20)

7. What points in David's prayer impress you (1 Chron. 29:10–13)?

List the attributes of God for which David gives praise. What emotions and attitudes did these thoughts about God bring forth in David (vv. 14–17)?

What prayer did David make for the people (29:17, 18)?

What did he request for Solomon (v. 19)?

8. Describe the scene in 1 Chronicles 29:20.

Examining your own heart: What brings the most sincere and deepest worship of God from you?

Thinking back over our study, why, do you think, was David called a man after God's own heart?

*I*t's a thrill to read how David spent his last days. They were filled with activity and excitement, for God gave him the task of collecting and preparing the materials for the magnificent temple his son Solomon would build. David had wanted to be the one to build the temple himself, and it seemed to everyone around that he was the appropriate person to do it, even to Nathan the prophet. But as we discovered in an earlier chapter (2 Sam. 7), God told Nathan to inform David this was not to be, and his son Solomon who would succeed him would have that privilege. At that time God gave David such astounding promises for the future of his kingdom that, instead of being angry and disappointed, David's heart overflowed with gratitude and praise. How gracious of God to give David the assurance that his idea for a temple was a good one, and to give him this hope. It meant David had a compelling purpose the rest of his life; for as wealth and riches accumulated, he carefully put much of it aside for the future dream. Think of the joy it gave David in his closing days to plan and prepare for the beautiful temple and to guide and instruct his son Solomon for the role and responsibilities of being king of Israel.

You remember from 2 Samuel 7 and the discussion on it why it was very important to David to construct a temple. David was aware of how Hebrew life had changed since the early days when God directed Moses to build the tabernacle. It had been a symbol of God's presence, of his constant love and concern for his people, and was constructed in such a way that it could be moved about with them. It was God's way of giving those early believers a visible symbol so they could grasp his reality. It was a place where he revealed himself to them, a place where they could come for the rituals of cleansing and forgiveness, where they could confess their sins both individually and nationally, and where they could renew their relationships with God. David did not want any of this concept lost; and now that Israel had a capital city containing great edifices, he was not happy that the most important structure of all was dwarfed and insignificant in comparison. Should not the most beautiful building of all be a temple where God could be worshiped and praised—a glorious symbol that God was in the heart and at the center of the national life?

It is interesting that God encouraged David in the project and carefully directed him in making plans for the temple, just as he had done for Moses when the original tabernacle was built. Evidently, God gave David every minute detail. When you think of the significance of each part, think of what a thrill it was for David to be taught all of this by God himself. That kind of information needed to be given to a man such as David, who knew God as perhaps few men have ever known him. David could appreciate the importance and meaning behind the symbols, and when he didn't understand, he obeyed anyway, knowing God had his own reasons. He was so thoroughly convinced that God had led him to begin this glorious task, which Solomon would complete, that his energy and efforts were totally directed to this project in the closing days of his life. Isn't this a beautiful example to us of how a "man after God's own heart" does not let down in his later years, but enthusiastically keeps on being useful to God until his last breath and final bit of energy? David's spiritual maturity was invaluable at this point and, as he made plans and collected materials, he could visualize the structure and sense the realization of his lifelong dream.

A Change in Leadership

The smooth transfer of power from David to Solomon is recounted most fully in 1 and 2 Chronicles, as well as details about the construction of the temple. Imagine the scene vividly pictured in 1 Chronicles 28, as David called together all of the leaders of the country, not just a few top men (v. 1). There were local city officials, leaders of the tribes, military officers, palace guards, and his own brave warriors, all brought together to hear about the exciting events that were to follow. No wonder they loved David! He didn't operate in back rooms with a few "yes men." David had already given these words to Solomon (1 Chron. 22), but he wanted all of the people to feel they were a part of this important event in Israel's life.

With Solomon at his side, the first thing David did was to inform the people that God had revealed to him that of all of his sons, Solomon was the one chosen to succeed him as king. Have you thought how gracious God was to let this son of David and Bathsheba be the next king? What a beautiful way for God to show what kind of God he is—one who can completely forgive. How grateful David and Bathsheba must have been that God indeed buried their sin in the depths of the sea, and did not hold their sin against their son!

> King David rose to his feet and said, "Listen to me, my brothers and my people. I had it in my heart to build a house as a place of rest for the ark of the covenant of the Lord, for the footstool of our God, and I made plans to build it. But God said to me, 'You are not to build a house for my Name, because you are a warrior and have shed blood.' Yet the Lord, the God of Israel, chose me from my whole family to be king over Israel forever. . . . Of all my sons . . . he has chosen my son Solomon to sit on the throne. . . . '[He] is the one who will build my house and my courts. . . . I will establish his kingdom forever if he is unswerving in carrying out my

commands and laws, as is being done at this time'" (1 Chron. 28:2–7).

David was so open and honest! It must have made the people feel very tender toward their beloved king to have him share his disappointment, but also to see his beautiful, humble attitude of acceptance and his joy at helping in the way God prescribed.

The Charge to the People

David wanted the people to catch his burning desire to build the temple, and wanted them to give as much help in its construction as they possibly could. How contagious his enthusiasm must have been when he said:

> So now I charge you in the sight of all Israel and of the assembly of the LORD, and in the hearing of our God: Be careful to follow all the commands of the LORD your God, that you may possess this good land and pass it on as an inheritance . . . forever (1 Chron. 28:8).

David pointed out that the land was very important; that God himself had chosen it and had given them the land of Israel, thereby keeping the promise made to their forefathers. Through many trials and great hardships God had enabled them to claim and occupy it and eventually become a nation. Now the responsibility was theirs to keep it intact for their children and grandchildren. However, the condition of God's blessing was, as it had always been, to "be careful to follow his commands." These precepts had been given by God out of love and for their own benefit, and David encouraged the people to follow all that God had said. We see in David's mind that the promise of an eternal kingdom was very real, "an inheritance forever."

As David looked out at the sea of faces before him, he felt great concern for them. He knew that one of the greatest disasters that could befall Israel would be if her king strayed from following the Lord God. David had ruled with his antenna finetuned to God, letting God lead, not just in words but in reality. He knew how busy and distracting a king's life would be, and how hard it was for a leader to maintain a close, personal communion with God. No doubt some of his own tragic mistakes loomed in his mind, and he longed to spare Solomon from falling into the same traps. Can you imagine David's thoughts as he dug deep into his heart and longed to share with his young son some of the wisdom God had given him in his forty years as king?

The Charge to Solomon

When David turned to his son, the atmosphere must have been electric with drama and emotion as he tried to distill into a few words the essence of what Solomon must do to carry out the awesome tasks of leading the people and building the beautiful temple. In the presence of all the people, David gave his charge to Solomon, which contained six specific points:

> And you, Solomon my son, know the God of your father, and serve him with a whole heart and with a willing mind; for the LORD searches all hearts and understands every plan and thought. If you seek him, he will be found by you; but if you forsake him, he will cast you off for ever. Take heed now, for the LORD has chosen you to build a house for a sanctuary; be strong and do it (1 Chron. 28:9, 10 RSV).

1. Know God. David's first thought was that above all else Solomon must concentrate on knowing God. He wanted this written on the tables of Solomon's heart—never to be forgotten—that he not just know *about* God but that he *know* God. The word *know* in this context means "to discern, to understand," rather than "to make known." The apostle Paul states that his greatest desire was that he would get to know Christ, not just know about him:

> I consider everything a loss compared to the surpassing greatness of knowing Christ Jesus my Lord, for whose sake I have lost all things. I consider them rubbish, that I may gain Christ, and be found in him. . . . I want to know Christ and the power of his resurrection and the fellowship of sharing in his sufferings, becoming like him in his death (Phil. 3:8, 10).

Think of all the love, unselfishness, obedience to God, and countless other qualities exhibited by Christ when he voluntarily submitted to death on the cross! Paul wanted to know and understand Christ so well that he would begin to be like him in that way.

Wasn't David saying the same thing? As he looked back over his life and thought of what Solomon would face, he was struck with the fact that the most important thing in his own life was getting to know and appreciate God, discovering him as he truly is—his attributes, his purposes and plans, his ways, and his desires for his children. Discovering these things about God were David's greatest joys, and this is what he most wanted to bequeath to his son. He urged Solomon to make knowing God his top priority.

2. Serve God with a whole heart. Notice how David focused first on God himself, and then on commitment to God, recognizing that true service flows out of a heart that knows and loves God as he is. Such service is not just keeping up a flurry of activity and being very busy doing good things; that may be service, but not necessarily service to God. David was talking about actions that come from a deep love for God, that come from deep inside. It is amazing how often David speaks of the heart and the inner man. One suspects that Samuel shared with David the fact that God had chosen him because of his heart (1 Sam. 16:7), since he spoke of it so often. Serving God "with a whole heart" speaks to a person's commitment or choice as to where the energy of his or her life is to go.

3. Serve God with a willing mind. David was dealing with the whole person. Not only must we know God and commit ourselves to him, but the attitude is all-important. David wanted Solomon to serve God willingly and joyfully, not grudgingly or out of a sense of duty. The psalmist wrote: "Make a joyful noise unto the LORD. . . . Serve the LORD with gladness: come before his presence with singing" (Ps. 100:1, 2 KJV). Similarly, in the New Testament we read, "Whatever you do, whether in word or deed, do it all in the name of the Lord Jesus, giving thanks to God the Father" (Col. 3:17).

4. Serve with a heart of pure motives. David was keenly aware that God looked into the deepest recesses of his heart. He knew that God required inward purity, not outward gestures. We can be performing good, unselfish acts outwardly, but when making choices and decisions we need to check the real reason we are doing things. The purest of motives have a way of shifting and can be replaced with our desires to be thought successful, seen as outstanding spiritual leaders, or to be in control. God sees such shifts, and can help us to get back to serving him with our whole hearts. What do your choices about the allocation of your time, energy, and resources show about your main concerns?

5. Seek God. David lived by prayer. He had led the nation by prayer, and he deeply desired that Solomon would give prayer its necessary and rightful place in his life. David had learned to seek God and he knew that he could ask God to show him his will, not only for himself, but for the nation. He had learned that prayer was a relationship, a time of communication expressing praise, thanksgiving, and joy to God—a time of receiving the quiet assurance that God had heard him and was expressing his love and thoughts back to him.

6. *Be strong and do the work!* The final thing David told Solomon was very practical. He told Solomon that the Lord had chosen him to lead in this task, and it was time to muster his courage and strength and begin. Can't you hear the father talking to the son, "Don't put it off! The materials are ready, the workmen and craftsmen are eager to start. Now get on with it, son." David also encouraged Solomon later in the chapter, "Do not be afraid or discouraged" (1 Chron. 28:20). He assured Solomon that God would be with him until the work was finished.

Isn't it easy to procrastinate? So often I have agreed to do a task, but then found all kinds of reasons to put it off. David was convinced that the strategic time to start the temple had arrived. What an encourager David was! Do you do this for people? David's faith rested squarely on his knowledge of what God was like, and he knew that God would delight in giving strength and stamina to Solomon for this task.

Choosing the Site for the Temple

It seems that plans for the temple began in earnest once David had purchased the plot of land he had become convinced was the ideal site. (Read this fascinating story in 1 Chronicles 21.) For some unknown reason, as David was nearing the end of his life, he fell into the serious sin of taking an elaborate census of his fighting men, which God had specifically told them not to do, since God wanted the king and the people always to trust in him rather than in the size of their army. Even Joab knew it was wrong, but he couldn't dissuade David. After some serious consequences for Israel, God told David to go to the threshing floor of Araunah the Jebusite, erect an altar there, and make sacrifices for his sin. David purchased the plot of ground from Araunah and carried out God's commands. God accepted David's contrite spirit and true repentance in a spectacular way. Because of this, David was convinced that the temple should be erected there. This particular site had great significance for Israel, because some eight hundred years earlier another altar had been erected there by Abraham. In obedience to God's command, Abraham would have offered his son Isaac to God on that altar but God intervened. On this very spot the magnificent temple was eventually built.

> Then David said, "The house of the LORD God is to be here, and also the altar of burnt offering for Israel." So David . . . appointed stonecutters to prepare dressed stone for building the house of God. He provided a large amount of iron to make nails for the doors of the gateways and for the fittings, and more bronze than could be weighed . . . more cedar logs than could be counted. . . . "The house to be built for the LORD should be of great magnificence and fame and splendor in the sight of all the nations. Therefore I will make preparations for it." So David made extensive preparations before his death. Then he called his son Solomon and charged him to build a house for the LORD, the God of Israel (1 Chron. 22:1–6).

Construction Plans and Preparations

David was most eager that Solomon catch the vision for this special task. He assured his son he would give him every bit of help that he possibly could, as well as support him with his constant prayers that God would guide every step of the way. What a heritage Solomon had!

It boggles our minds to think of God giving David such detailed plans for the temple. How did he do it? We can only imagine the hours David must have spent on his knees, seeking God's direction for each design and asking God to give him strength and energy to do all he must do. He probably consulted expert builders to procure the perfect materials for each item, and asked for suggestions for skilled workmen and artisans. Add architect to David's other accomplishments! Can you picture the scene as David turned the plans over to Solomon? They must have spent many days going over the plans together while David excitedly explained exactly what God told him should be done:

> Then David gave his son Solomon the plans for the portico of the temple, its buildings, its storerooms, its upper parts, its inner rooms and the place of atonement. He gave him the plans of all that the Spirit had put in his mind for the courts of the temple of the LORD and all the surrounding rooms. . . . He gave him instructions for the divisions of the priests and Levites. . . . He designated . . . the articles to be used in the various kinds of service . . . lampstands . . . tables . . . forks . . . bowls and pitchers . . . the cherubim of gold that spread their wings and shelter the ark of the covenant. . . . "All this is in writing," David said, "because the hand of the LORD was upon me and gave me understanding in all the details of the plan" (1 Chron. 28:11–19).

Amazing! He even designated the exact weights of the gold and silver to be used for each item, down to the weight of the last silver dish.

The Challenge to Begin Building the Temple

David repeated his challenge to Solomon:

> Be strong and courageous and do the work. Do not be afraid or discouraged, for the LORD God, my God, is with you. He will not fail or forsake you until all the work for the service of the temple of the LORD is finished. The divisions of the priests and Levites are ready for all the work on the temple of God, and every willing man skilled in any craft will help you in all the work. The officials and all the people will obey your every command (1 Chron. 28:20, 21).

David had not only prepared the plans and gathered the materials for constructing the temple, but he also presented to Solomon willing and skilled workers, ready to begin the work.

Then David must have looked at his young son, who was perhaps seventeen years old at the time, a boy who had been "born with a silver spoon in his mouth," not yet tempered by experience and strengthened by suffering as David had been when he took the throne from Saul. David saw the dangers ahead. It was a poignant moment when he turned to the people and appealed to them to give the young Solomon their full support and help:

> My son Solomon, the one whom God has chosen, is young and inexperienced. The task is great because this palatial structure is not for man but for the LORD God. With all my resources I have provided for the temple of my God (1 Chron. 29:1, 2).

David enumerated the large quantities of materials he was contributing, not to brag or show off but to emphasize that his heart was truly in this endeavor. Even his personal treasures of gold and silver were gladly given. The custom in that day would have been to use these treasures to finance some magnificent memorial to himself so he would be remembered as a great king. Perhaps a spectacular tomb, a pyramid, or some great monument would have been appropriate, but David's devotion to the temple of the Lord was so great that he wanted all of his wealth to be poured into it.

After showing his own commitment to the project, David turned to the people and said, "Now, who is willing to consecrate himself today to the Lord?" The people were so overcome by David's enormous generosity at this point that they followed his example. The leaders started it off by giving willingly and generously. Then "The people rejoiced at the willing response of their leaders, for they had given freely and wholeheartedly to the LORD. David the king also rejoiced greatly" (1 Chron 29:9). With the people's response, David's emotions overflowed into prayer and praise. He led the people in rejoicing in the greatness of God and in enumerating different facets of the character of his eternal God, who had meant everything to him and had given him everything he had. He insisted that all of the glory and the praise go to God (1 Chron. 29:10–13). As David saw it, he and the nation now had the great privilege of giving back to God what God had given to them! Isn't it wonderful how God gave David the strength to be such a vigorous and effective leader to the very end of his life?

Contributions and Legacy of David

What an amazing spectacle it was when David turned his kingdom over to Solomon in the presence of all the leaders of the country. Think of the legacy he left Solomon and Israel. Israel's enemies had been subdued and the country was at peace. The borders had been vastly extended, so there was a sense of safety and security as well as prosperity. Internally, the government was well-organized and running smoothly. The people were excited about their country, were eager to participate in its national life, and proud to be a part of their nation. Foreign relations had never been better, and Israel was now considered one of the "super powers" of the Middle East. David had made it a joy to be counted as one of God's people. What a kingdom Solomon inherited! Most important of all, the people were excited about God and what he had done through David. David had not amassed gold and silver so that Israel could flaunt her wealth before other nations; neither was it for Solomon to inherit and squander personally, and the people caught that attitude.

What a capacity for joy David had, even to the end of his days! He was probably over seventy years old and had lost much of his physical strength when he turned the throne over to Solomon. But he was not a grumpy, bitter old man. He could still praise God and rejoice vigorously, and lead others in doing so. He still wrote songs to be used for praise. He wrote joyous prayers of thanksgiving, as well as prayers for all occasions. He was himself a beautiful example of a person who gave wholeheartedly of his talents and resources to God—joyfully, humbly, and with total devotion.

As we read of these final events in David's life, how he turned the kingdom over to Solomon and encouraged him and the people to keep God at the center of their private and public lives, much is revealed about the kind of man David was. When he gave the blueprints for the temple to Solomon, we read, "He gave him the plans of all that the Spirit had put in his mind" (1 Chron. 28:12), and "'All this is in writing,' David said, 'because the hand of the LORD was upon me, and he gave me an understanding in all the details of the plan'" (v. 19). These words are another clue to help us understand what it means to be "a man after God's own heart." David allowed God, through the Holy Spirit, to write his plans and his will on his mind, and through this, to imprint his own character in David's heart. David's prayer was that this be a continuing process: "Create in me a pure heart . . . renew a steadfast spirit within me . . . Grant me a willing spirit" (Ps. 51:10, 12). God answered that prayer, and for this reason God could use David powerfully to the end of his days, and beyond.

Christ Jesus, David's Eternal Legacy

David had wanted to build a house for God, but God said, "the LORD himself will establish a house for you. Your house and your kingdom will endure forever before me; your throne will be established forever" (2 Sam. 7:11, 16). David was overwhelmed when God gave him that promise. Of course he didn't understand it all, but he understood enough to catch some of the glory of it. As plans for the temple began to materialize, David somehow sensed that the temple was foreshadowing something God was planning for his people in the future. David's earthly kingdom began to crumble within fifty years after his death, but God's promise to him was gloriously fulfilled when Jesus Christ, David's descendant, came into the world to be our Savior. The temple—its furnishings, the sacrifices and ceremonies, the priesthood—all pointed to Christ (Heb. 9). Although God had given David the ability to write down what he learned about him and his character, there was to come after David one of his descendants who would be the perfect revelation of God, the embodiment of God's nature and character in human form. John wrote concerning Jesus, "The Word was made flesh and dwelt among us, (and we beheld his glory, the glory as of the only begotten of the Father), full of grace and truth" (John 1:14 KJV).

It is amazing how many times the Bible points out that Christ was David's descendant. When the angel announced to Mary that she was chosen by God to bring forth a son, Gabriel said, "He will be great and will be called the Son of the Most High. The Lord God will give him the throne of his father David" (Luke 1:32). The apostle Paul summarized David's life in an amazing statement that underscores David's importance in the plans and purposes of God:

> After removing Saul, he [God] made David their king. He testified concerning him: "I have found David son of Jesse a man after my own heart; he will do everything I want him to do." From this man's descendants God has brought to Israel the Savior Jesus, as he promised (Acts 13:22, 23).

The enduring kingdom God promised to David was clearly that of Christ, which would be everlasting, and the city that David conquered and made his capital foreshadowed the new Jerusalem mentioned in Revelation:

Then I saw a new heaven and a new earth. . . . I saw the
Holy City, the new Jerusalem, coming down out of heaven
from God, prepared as a bride beautifully dressed for her
husband. And I heard a loud voice from the throne saying,
"Now the dwelling of God is with men, and he will live with
them. They will be his people, and God himself will be with
them and be their God" (Rev. 21:1–3). I am the Root and the
Offspring of David, and the bright Morning Star (Rev. 22:16).

As we come to the close of our study, David's prayer in 1
Chronicles 29 is a most fitting ending. David's whole focus
in this prayer was on God, and David's love and appreciation for all that God was to him poured forth from his heart
as he praised God for the marvelous attributes of his character. Would you rejoice and praise, along with David, our
wonderful sovereign Lord?

> Praise be to you, O LORD,
>> God of our father Israel,
>> from everlasting to everlasting.
> Yours, O LORD, is the greatness and the power
>> and the glory and the majesty and the splendor,
>> for everything in heaven and earth is yours.
> Yours, O LORD, is the kingdom;
>> you are exalted as head over all.
> Wealth and honor come from you;
>> you are the ruler of all things.
> In your hands are strength and power
>> to exalt and give strength to all.
> Now, our God, we give you thanks,
>> and praise your glorious name (1 Chron. 29:10–13).

7

God Inspires David, the Praying Poet

Primary Scripture Reading

Psalm 18

Supplementary References

2 Samuel 22
Psalm 19:1, 14; 24:1, 2, 10;
    25:7, 18; 32:3–6; 36:5, 7;
    51:5, 6; 124
Galatians 3:6–9
Philippians 2:14–16

Questions for Study and Discussion

1. Read Psalm 18 and scan 2 Samuel 22. Read over all the following questions. Looking at the whole psalm, try to pair up incidents from David's life that you remember with the different ideas expressed in Psalm 18.

2. List the different emotions you find communicated by the psalmist, both negative and positive.

3. What characteristics and names are given for God in verses 1, 2, 30 and 46?

Explain why each one was important to David, and why they are important to you.

Relate some recent experiences when God showed these qualities to you.

4. Try to visualize the pictures described in verses 4–19.

Find some examples of "parallelism" (the practice of repeating or expanding the same idea in different words in the next line or phrase).

How does the imagery in verses 7–19 relate to verses 3 and 6?

5. In verses 20–29 how does David describe himself?

Is he egotistical?

What do you think he means by his "righteousness" and his "clean hands"? (for your answer compare with Psalm 25:7, 18; 32:3–6; 57:5, 6, and Philippians 2:14–16).

6. Who, do you think, were David's enemies mentioned in verses 3, 14, 37–48?

Should a godly man speak this way about anyone?

List some of your enemies—not people, but tendencies or influences which hinder you from being victorious over sin.

Choose some poetic images from verses 20–37 which suggest ways to deal with these destructive forces.

7. List (with references) the times David exercised his will in Psalm 18 and the deliberate choices and resolutions he made.

8. For a bonus blessing, use this psalm for your devotions, praying and praising along with David. Recount specific times when God has delivered you, given strength, or inspired trust. Paraphrase to suit your own situations.

*V*ery early this morning I slipped out of our apartment on Sanibel Island to take my usual morning walk along the Gulf. The beach was a delicate coral as the first suggestions of light were appearing, and salmon-colored rays were skittering across the water and onto the shiny wet sand. A few early shell seekers poked around in the tide, and an energetic jogger loped by. But my attention was riveted on the breathtaking things happening on the horizon. The dark sky, still dotted with a few persistent stars, was fading into gray. Fluffy clouds were becoming visible, and were reflecting the reds and corals beginning to appear where the sky meets the water. The stars were fast disappearing, and as more light came the sky became bluer, transforming the reds into a deep magenta, soon fading into a glowing pink, then a soft apricot, and finally a brilliant gold. A tiny glowing arc emerged as though out of the water, and in a few moments the full sun was too bright to watch. As I gazed at that glorious display over the water, for well over a half-hour, I wanted desperately to freeze each moment in my memory. But more than that, I kept wanting to express to God my delight in his handiwork, my gratitude for his beautiful creation, my thanks for his faithfulness. The sheer joy of being his child flooded my being just as light had flooded the scene, but my attempts to put my feelings into my own words seemed shallow and insipid. The words I found myself saying were words from the psalms, words I had learned from the King James version as a child.

O LORD, our LORD, how excellent is thy name in all the earth! who has set thy glory above the heavens (Ps. 8:1).

The heavens declare the glory of God; and the firmament showeth his handiwork (Ps. 19:1).

The earth is the LORD's, and the fullness thereof; the world, and they that dwell therein. For he hath founded it upon the seas, and established it upon the floods . . . Who is the King of glory? the LORD strong and mighty, he is the King of glory (Ps. 24:1, 2, 10).

Thy mercy, O LORD, is in the heavens; and thy faithfulness reacheth to the clouds . . . How excellent is thy lovingkindness, O God! Therefore the children of men put their trust under the shadow of thy wings (Ps. 36:5, 7).

I knew just how the psalmist felt when he wrote, "O that men would praise the LORD for his goodness, and for his wonderful works to the children of men:" (Ps. 107:15 KJV). I wanted to shout these words to people as they walked by! I think of many other times in my life when words from the psalms have come to mind, or have jumped out of the printed page and expressed for me my thoughts and emotions. As different experiences have brought with them their own set of emotions—sometimes exuberant joy, sometimes frustration and confusion, sometimes pain and sorrow, invariably the psalmist's words have fit exactly.

Vivid in my memory is one night twelve years ago when the phone rang, and our oldest daughter, then mother of four children, told us she had just received a devastating report from her doctor. He had detected breast cancer. I recall clearly how at first I was too stunned to pray. I couldn't put anything meaningful into words, but after a time, I almost forced myself to get on my knees. I opened up my Bible to the psalms, and like familiar and loving friends, they enfolded and embraced me, and pointed my heart toward God. They enabled me to begin communicating with him. Through the psalms, he assured me that this news was no surprise to him, that he was in control, and he was right in the midst of our trouble with us. We were not alone. I will never forget the times my daughter and I had together before the surgery, as she found an almost uncanny peace and calm as we read various psalms together. She clung especially to Psalm 18, and remarked with awe, "I can't believe that David felt exactly as I do. Read on, Mom." God made his love and presence very real in that hospital room. Just as David loved to dwell on the ways God had blessed him in the past, often recalling events from many years before, our family loves to recall such experiences. We find ourselves recounting and analyzing just what God did for us, and praising God anew for his presence.

There are many ways to study the psalms, but however we do it, it is good to remember we are reading Hebrew poetry. The King James Version of the psalms stands out as superb literature, and if you love poetry as I do, you can be greatly moved simply by the beauty of the language. A careful study of its distinctive characteristics can be fascinating and rewarding. Hebrew scholars can unfold for us the structure and symmetry, as well as the rhythmic patterns and nuances that may be lost in translation. One of the most obvious characteristics of the psalms, even to the layman, is the use of *parallelism* (the practice of repeating the same idea in different words, usually in the next line or phrase). This balanced construction, not lost in our English versions, greatly enriches and enhances the psalms for the Christian. An idea is expressed, then expanded and embroidered so that if one phrase doesn't hit home, the next one may. Often our needs and fears are laid bare, and our hidden emotions and weaknesses are exposed. Psychologists tell us it is healthy for us to get in touch with our feelings, to take them out and look at them, name them and own up to them. The psalms have a striking way of helping us do just that.

We can be reasonably certain that Psalm 18 was written by David. Not only is it ascribed to him, but we find it corresponds closely to 2 Samuel 22, which opens with these words: "David sang to the LORD the words of this song." In colorful imagery, David takes us through his emotions and thought patterns. He is deeply grateful that God has proved to him over and over that he is all that he claimed to be: flawless and unchanging, loving and powerful. He elaborated on the various ways God, at vital times in his life, demonstrated that he was his rock, his fortress, his deliverer, his shield, his savior, and his stronghold. This song was probably sung by Israel on many occasions, either to praise for some recent deliverance, or at the regular temple services.

Someone has aptly entitled this psalm, "the outpouring of a heart to God." David frequently exhorted God's people to "pour out your hearts to God," and in Psalm 18 we find David doing just that. It is a marvelous demonstration of David's approach to God, and the way he laid out and verbalized his feelings and perceptions in prayer also teaches us to pray. When we use the psalms in a devotional and personal way, praising with them, confessing, voicing our petitions to God through them, we are on solid ground, for the greatest Christian scholars and theologians tell us they have learned to pray in this way. After Augustine was converted, he was advised by the church fathers to use only the psalms as his prayers for two years—then he would know how to pray. In his *Confessions* (ix. 4) he wrote: "How I addressed you, my God, in those psalms! How my love for you was kindled by them, and how I burned to recite them, if I could, throughout the world to oppose the pride of mankind!"

David's Deliberate Choices

> I will love thee, O LORD, my strength.
> The LORD is my rock, and my fortress, and my deliverer; my God, my strength, in whom I will trust; my buckler, and the horn of my salvation, and my high tower.
> I will call upon the LORD, who is worthy to be praised: so shall I be saved from mine enemies (Psalm 18:1–3 KJV).

It is surprising how often David's will was involved in his relationship with God, and how he deliberately set his mind to adopt certain attitudes and actions, and to bring his mind into harmony with the plans and character of God. (See Ps. 19:14; 139:17, 23, 24). He lets us witness his struggle as he often seems to be carrying on a conversation within his inner being, urging himself to validate the authenticity of his faith by acting on what he knows to be true. He wrote, "My heart says of you, 'Seek his face!' Your face, LORD, will I seek" (Ps. 27:8).

David was determined to be totally honest with God about his circumstances, his feelings, and his failure and successes. In his talks with God, we see David consciously choosing praise instead of self-pity, joy instead of gloom, and dependence on God's wisdom instead of groping for his own solutions. We sense that he almost forces himself to accept encouragement, strength, and guidance. After he makes these conscious decisions, he bursts forth into joyous praise and release. We see this process in psalm after psalm.

In the first line of Psalm 18, David makes the deliberate choice to love God. He refused to come to God with a cold heart, for in David's mind God deserved warm, personal devotion, the same loving affection parents feel for their children and loving spouses feel for each other. Prayer for David was not just a formal reciting of words of thanks for what God had done, followed by a list of what he wanted him to do next. Jesus, quoting from the Old Testament, said the greatest commandment is, "Love the LORD your God with all your heart and with all of your soul and with all your strength and with all your mind" (Deut. 6:5; Lev. 19:18). David reveals through his poetry that he understood those words, for his relationship to God involved his total self, his emotions, his will, his intellect, and his physical strength.

David repeatedly made decisions and vows to act in certain ways. For instance, he determined to give up fear. When he found himself in dire circumstances which would terrify any man, he made these declarations: "I will not fear" (Ps. 3:3). "Though an army besiege me, my heart will not fear" (Ps. 27:3). "Even though I walk through the shadow of death, I will fear no evil, for you are with me" (Ps. 23:4). In Psalm 69 he describes his feelings of discouragement and depression so graphically we almost feel his pain with him. He is hated, mistreated, alienated, disgraced, heartbroken, ashamed, and besides all that, he is physically exhausted and spiritually depleted. He wrote, "I am worn out calling for help; my throat is parched, my eyes fail, looking for my God" (Ps. 69:3). For twenty-nine verses he describes his miserable circumstance, begging God to do something. Then David seems to pull himself together and discipline his mind and heart, for he goes on to make this resolve: "I will praise God's name in song and glorify him with thanksgiving . . . This will please the LORD . . . The poor will see and be glad—you who seek God, may your hearts live" (vv. 30–32; see also Ps. 13).

David's words, spoken in the midst of deep discouragement drive us to recount the ways God has shown us his special love in the past, given us strength and comfort, and infused us with praise and even song. With David, and with men and women down through the ages we declare, "I will praise you, O LORD, with all my heart. I will tell of all your wonders. I will be glad and rejoice in you; I will sing praise to your name" (Ps. 9:1–2).

Paul, like David, encourages us to make a conscious decision to bring our minds in tune with God. He said to believers: "Since you have been risen with Christ, *set your affection* on things above, not on things of the earth" (Col. 3:2 KJV). He also counseled new converts to deliberately *think* on things that are pure, right, excellent, and praiseworthy (Phil. 4:8), and to "take captive every thought to make it obedient to Christ" (2 Cor. 10:5). Paul, like David, reminds us to choose to rejoice, regardless of circumstances (Phil. 4:4 and Col. 1:11). God can mold those who set their minds to follow these principles, and can use them to bless their generation and beyond, as he did David and Paul.

David's Distress and Desperation

> The cords of death entangled me;
> > the torrents of destruction overwhelmed me.
> The cords of the grave coiled around me;
> > the snares of death confronted me.
> In my distress I called to the LORD;
> > I cried to my God for help.
> From his temple he heard my voice;
> > my cry came before him, into his ears (vv. 3–6).

There were many crises in David's life which could have triggered these words, but according to the note preceding the psalm, it is praise for God's deliverance from enemies, especially from Saul. Saul continually plotted David's demise and pursued him aggressively for some fourteen years (1 Sam. 18:25; 20:33), at one point instructing almost his entire army to hunt him down (1 Sam. 23:8). Notice the poet's use of parallelism to reinforce the depth of his need. David felt helpless, as though he were entangled and ensnared in ropes, as if he were bound and could barely move, imprisoned with every way of escape blocked. We envision him being pulled down under torrents of water, yet he didn't bottle up his fears. He knew there was one gate left open to him—the gate of prayer. Our cry to God may be feeble, but we can be confident it is heard by God, and say, "My cry came before *him*, into *his* ears." It is heard not by his angels, or his chief emissaries, but by God himself.

David's Description of God's Display of Power

In my distress I called to the LORD; . . .
The earth trembled and quaked,
   and the foundations of the mountains shook; . . .
He parted the heavens and came down;
   dark clouds were under his feet.
He mounted the cherubim and flew;
   he soared on the wings of the wind. . . .
Out of the brightness of his presence clouds advanced,
   with hailstones and bolts of lightning. . . .
He shot his arrows and scattered the enemies,
   great bolts of lightning and routed them.
The valleys of the sea were exposed
   and the foundations of the earth laid bare (vv. 6–15).

When God's children call to him, he responds swiftly and effectively, and things begin to happen. With graphic pictures, David brings us into the tremendous force of a devastating electrical storm, an earthquake, or the awesome power of a violent hurricane, flash flood, or whirling tornado. Throughout the psalms we find God's character and actions described in cosmic terms, illustrated by the forces of nature—to help us worship him in his splendor, his vastness, and his sovereignty. Yet these pictures are usually coupled with a view of God's personal side, so we can grasp his concern and his nearness without losing any of the majestic wonder. Note how David shifts from the awesome display of power to a tender and intimate picture:

> He reached down from on high and took hold of me;
>   he drew me out of deep waters.
> He rescued me from my powerful enemy,
>   from my foes, who were too strong for me. . . .
> He brought me into a spacious place;
>   he rescued me because he delighted in me (vv. 16–19).

What a picture for us to hold in our minds! The drowning person is lovingly lifted out of the water, the confined prisoner is released and brought to a spacious place, for the God of the universe has reached down and become our rock, solid and unchangeable, our fortress and refuge, our shield and protector, our deliverer and savior—eager to respond because he delights in us, his children (v. 19).

When God rescued David, it was often from the pressure and distress caused by his enemies, both personal and national. What about David's attitude toward them? For us, living on this side of the cross and having a rich legacy of New Testament teachings, such thoughts as expressed in verses 3, 17, 18, and 37–48 seem out of character for the "man after God's own heart." They seem at odds with Christ's explicit instructions that we "turn the other cheek" when we are struck, and "love our enemies" no matter what they do to us (Matt. 5:39, 43, 44). In reading the psalms, it is good to remember David's unique role in establishing the Jewish nation, and the task God had given him—to expand and secure Israel's borders. This entailed almost constant military conflicts. In a very real sense, David saw his enemies as his nation's enemies and as God's enemies. He saw his victories as God's victories. He faithfully sought God's direction, obeyed him, and witnessed many magnificent things God did for him against great odds. David exhibited amazing skill as a military leader and was a brilliant strategist, but he had no illusions about who won those battles. He was aware that many times there would have been total disaster without God and saw to it that God got the praise for David's successes (2 Sam. 5:2, 7, 12, 20). David said to the people, "Let Israel say, 'If the LORD had not been on our side when men attacked us . . . they would have swallowed us alive; the flood would have engulfed us . . . Praise be to the LORD . . . Our help is in the name of the LORD'" (Ps. 124:1, 8).

Are David's words about his adversaries relevant to us today? Indeed they are. If we view these enemies in the psalms not as people, but as forces that are within us, these passages come alive for us. We can view them as influences that hinder God's will from being carried out through us, that thwart our being God's instruments in some strategic spot where he has placed us. Think of how the forces of evil seek to gain territory, set up strongholds in our lives, and keep us from reaching the potential God intends for us to reach through his Spirit. The psalms have a way of pinpointing our true enemies: laziness, coldness of heart, anger, resentment, depression, self-centeredness, lack of faith, lack of joy, neglect of the Bible, dullness of mind, failure to pray. The list goes on and on. As with David's enemies, God's mighty power can conquer these forces, can keep them from controlling our actions, and can even annihilate some of them. Dwelling on the character of God as David did, on God's grandeur, his power, his sovereignty, impels us to count on God to unleash that power against our enemies. When this happens, David's descriptions no longer seem overly grand and exaggerated. Instead, they hit the nail on the head, open our eyes to the ways God has already won victories for us, and initiate our praise for God's deliverance.

David's Disciplined Life and Clean Conscience

> The LORD has dealt with me according to my righteous-
> ness;
> according to the cleanness of my hands. . . .
> For I have kept the ways of the LORD;
> I have not done evil by turning from my God. . . .
> I have been blameless before him
> and have kept myself from sin.
> The LORD has rewarded me according to my righteous-
> ness,
> according to the cleanness of my hands in his sight.
> To the faithful you show yourself faithful,
> to the blameless you show yourself blameless,
> To the pure you show yourself pure (vv. 20–26).

Do these words strike you as egotistical? Paul writes in the same vein in this admonition, "Do everything without complaining or arguing, so that you may become blameless and pure, children of God without fault in a crooked and depraved generation, in which you shine as stars in the universe" (Phil. 2:14). Jesus himself, knowing full well what we are like, said, "Be perfect, as your heavenly father is perfect" (Matt. 5:48). Yet Paul considered himself as the "chief of sinners" (1 Tim. 1:15), and David follows with this statement: "You save the humble but bring low those whose eyes are haughty" (v. 27).

David, like Paul, makes clear many times that whatever righteousness he had, it did not come from his deeds or accomplishments. To him, the "cleanness of his hands" was something only God could give out of his abundant mercy, a gift he chose to accept. But David also felt the responsibility of conducting himself in such a way that others knew he was coming "with clean hands." In dealing with Saul, David was a beautiful example of Christ's New Testament standards as he refused to take revenge, to harbor bitterness, or to retaliate in any way for Saul's fanatical and unwarranted cruelty. David came to God with a clear conscience and clean hands in regard to Saul, and those around David knew it.

It is remarkable that a thousand years before Christ David caught much of the meaning of redemption and justification. Paul, in trying to explain how God imputes Christ's righteousness to us, wrote, "David says the same thing when he speaks of the blessedness of the man to whom God credits righteousness apart from works" (Rom. 4:6). Martin Luther said he found the basis of his faith in Romans and Galatians, but when he went to the Old Testament, particularly the psalms, he found the whole gospel in a nutshell. Calvin felt the same way, declaring that the whole faith of the whole Christian person can be found in the psalms.

In verses 20–25 we see a beautiful side of David. He wanted to come to his God with a pure heart. He had chosen "to keep the ways of the LORD" (v. 21), and to keep himself from sin (v. 23). God, to David, was not a benign doting grandfather who winked at sin. God was not his "buddy," or a "genie" who hopped to do David's bidding when he prayed, like the "genie" of Aladdin's magic lamp. Yet David, like Paul, had the strong conviction that God is "for us," and is eager to help us be victorious (Ps. 18:31, 32, 35; Rom. 8:31, 37). The next verses show us how God delivers us and enables us to overcome.

David's Deliverance and Triumph

> You, O LORD, keep my lamp burning;
> my God turns my darkness into light.

> With your help I can advance against a troop;
> with my God I can scale a wall. . . .
> It is God who arms me with strength
> and makes my way perfect.
> He makes my feet like the feet of a deer;
> he enables me to stand on the heights. . . .
> You broaden the path beneath me,
> so that my ankles do not turn (vv. 28–36).

In the beautiful and vivid imagery of the poet we see the things God wants to do and be for us. He turns our darkness into light so we don't have to grope and stumble. He wants to guide us, help us avoid the pitfalls, lead us to develop skills, and see that we make progress. We have the picture of David being given the agility and feet of a deer or mountain goat whose hooves cling to the side of the rocky cliffs so they can scale to dangerous heights and not slip. What an encouraging picture—a God who turns our exhaustion into energetic service, our discouragement into hope, our weakness into strength, and our faltering, slippery footsteps into surefootedness. We too can climb to great heights with no fear of falling. David felt that God had transformed his feet, his hands, his ankles, and his arms, literally and figuratively, as he fled from Saul. God did not remove Saul as David must have hoped he would, but instead broadened David's path and gave him places of security and rest. God also wants to do for us and help us accomplish things we never dreamed could be possible. Are these things happening in your life?

Psalm 18 ends with a look toward the future. Bearing in mind all that God has been to him and his people, David concludes:

> Therefore will I praise you among the nations, O Lord;
> I will sing praises to your name.
> He gives his king great victories;

he shows unfailing kindness to his anointed,
to David and his descendants forever (vv. 49, 50).

Christ is in that verse, and so are you and I. Christ is the
anointed Son of David, and those of us who believe in him
have been taken into God's family and are descendants of
David by adoption (Gal. 3:6–9). Through his perfect life,
his atoning death, and his glorious resurrection, Christ
accomplished the ultimate victory. God is constantly showing his unfailing kindness to us and will continue to do so
into eternity.

It is easy for us to believe that David and the other
psalmists were skillfully guided by the Holy Spirit as they
composed their poetry, even to the words they used. View-
ing God with David enlarges and expands our perception
of our Maker and deepens our faith. Confessing with David
helps us see our sin and accept God's gracious forgiveness.
Verbalizing our fears and perplexities with David helps us
release our burdens and grip the Lord's hand. Articulating
honestly our deepest thoughts and emotions with David
helps us bring God into all the details of our lives. Praising
with David helps us express to God our love, awe, and wonder. Singing with David gives us a joyful heart overflowing
with delight in our God.

Make the psalms your own! Absorb their wonderful
truths! Sing with them! Praise with them! Cry with them!
Pray with them! Paraphrase them in your own words using
your own imagery and parallelism. Believe that it delights
God to hear your voice, to accept your praise, and to answer
your cries for help.

Suggestions for Group Leaders

1. Keep in mind that the purpose of group discussion is to help all the members understand the Bible, implement the truths learned, refresh each other by exchanging thoughts, impressions, and ideas, and to support the formation of bonds of friendship.

2. Encourage the members to set aside a daily time for study and prayer.

3. Remind the members to write out answers. Expressing oneself on paper clarifies thoughts and analyzes understanding. Because written answers are succinct and thoughtful, discussion will be enlivened.

4. Be familiar enough with the lesson so you can identify questions that can most easily be omitted if time is short. Select and adapt an appropriate number of questions so that the lesson topic can be completed. Reword the question if the group feels it is unclear. Covering too little material is discouraging to the class. Skip the questions that cover material the class has already discussed. Often the last questions are the most thought-provoking. Choose questions that create lively and profitable interchange of views.

5. Encourage all members to participate. Often the less vocal people have amazingly thoughtful contributions.

6. Keep the group focused on the passage studied, emphasizing that answers should come from Scripture. Steer
the discussion away from tangents. Sidestep contro-
versial subjects, Christian causes, political action, and
so forth. Ask, "Where did you find that in this passage?"
"Did anyone find a thought not yet mentioned?"

7. Pick up on any "live news" of spiritual growth, recent
actions taken, honest admissions of inadequacy or failures, and desires for prayer. Be sensitive to "beginners"
in the Christian walk, recognizing their need to share
new discoveries, joys, commitments, and decisions.

8. Spend time in prayer as you prepare for the lesson.
Remember to pray for each member. Pray daily for your-
self to have a listening ear, a sensitive heart, and an
effervescent and contagious spirit of joy as you lead.
Pray you will affirm each member who contributes. Ask
God to give you a variety of ways to do this.

Closing Remarks

Prepared closing remarks are valuable (and essential) for
clearing up misunderstandings of the passage, further
teaching, applying the Scripture to current situations, and
for challenging each individual to action. Before the meeting decide on how much time to allow for discussion and
closing remarks, and follow the timetable.